AF326645

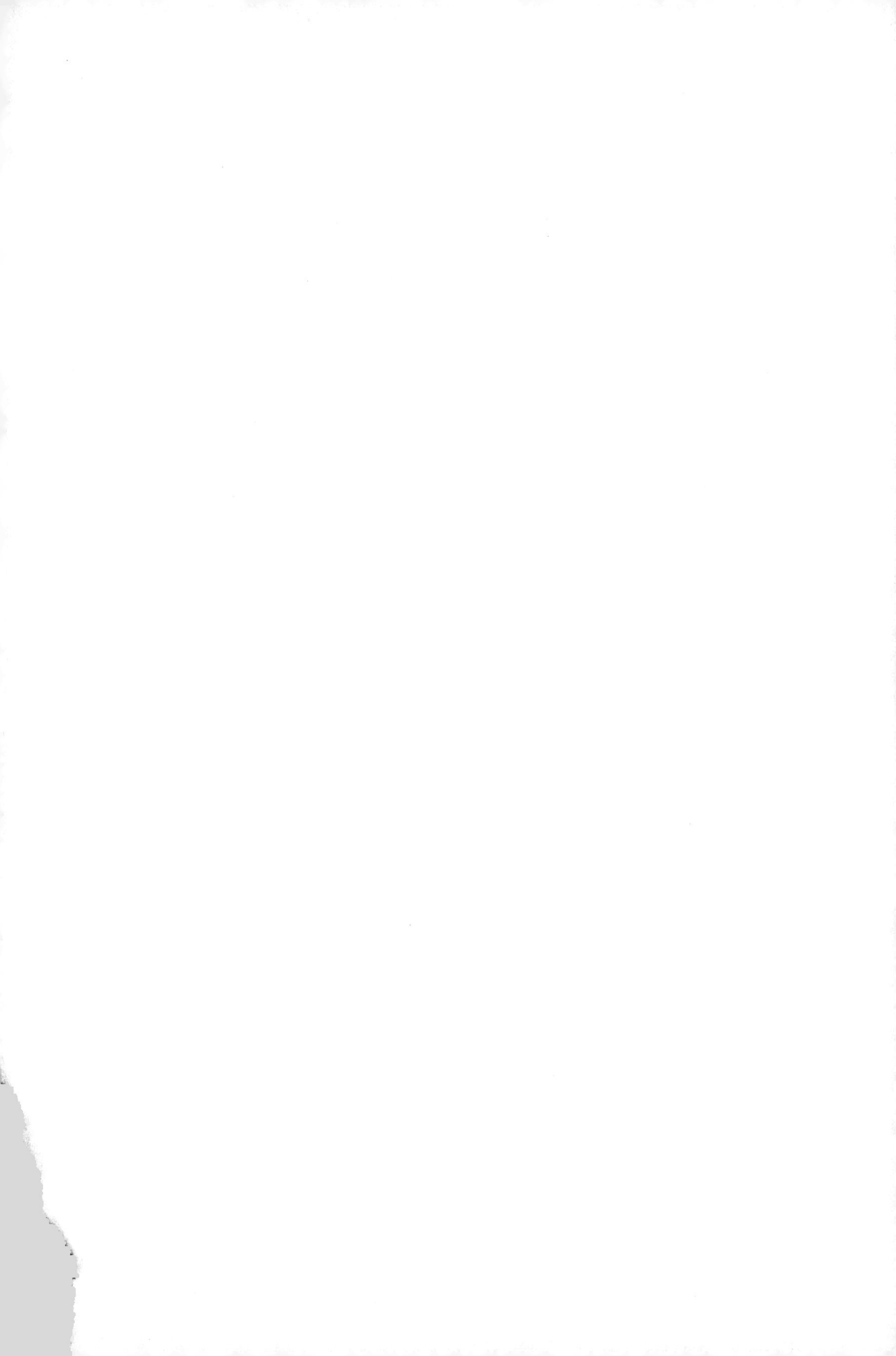

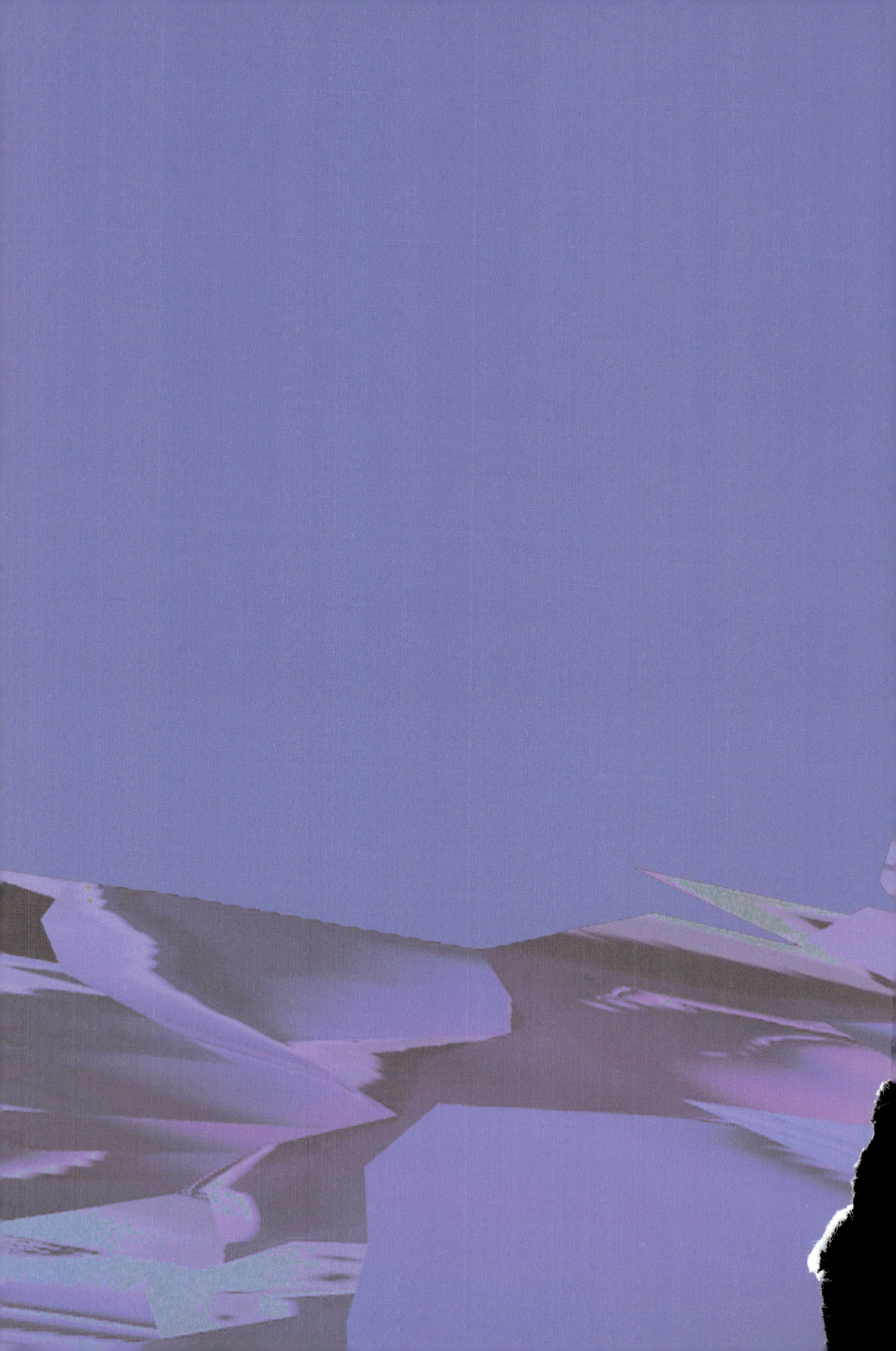

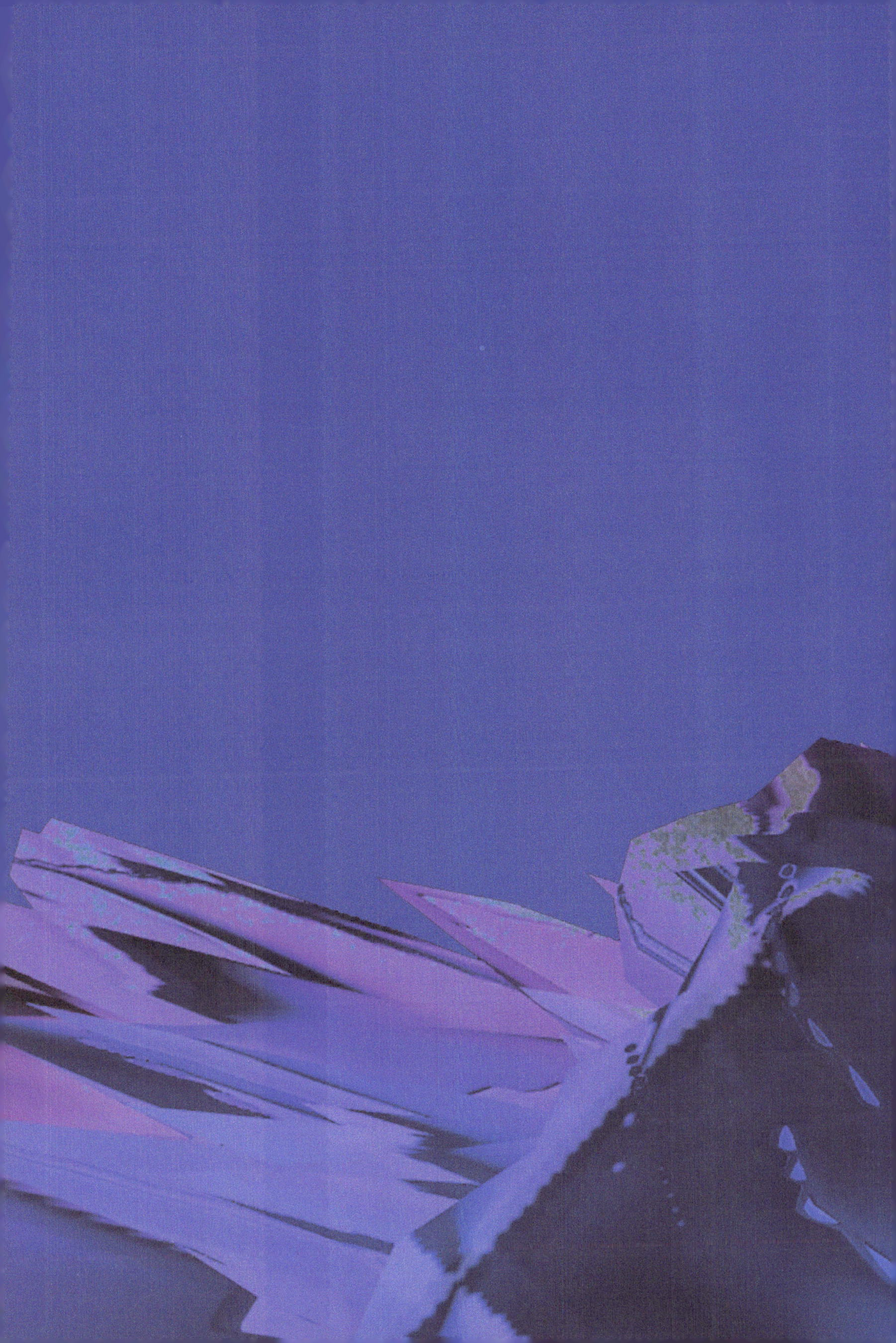

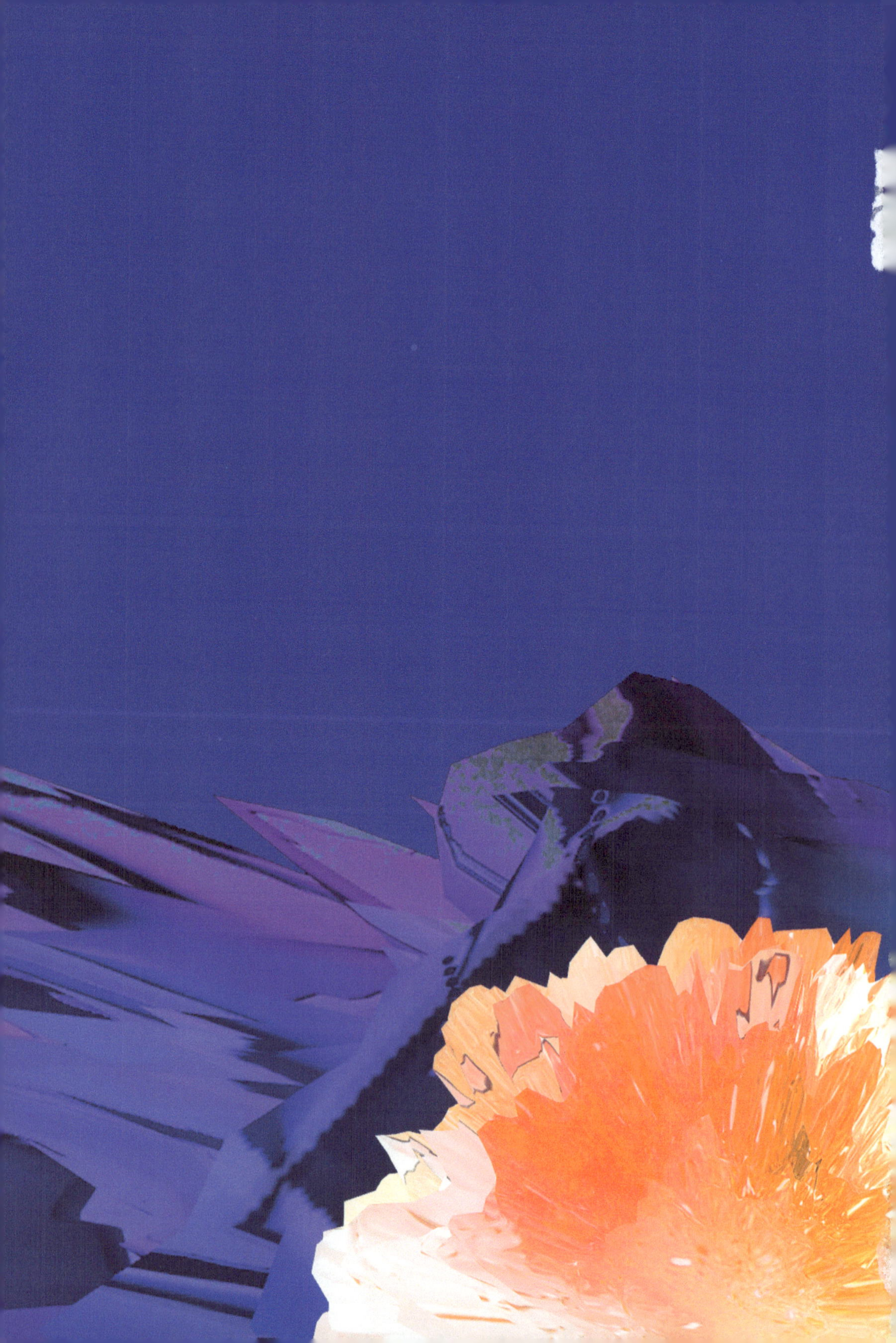

T O

12

B A

**The 12
Breaking Out
Animals**

To the new reality.

www.t12boa.com

The 12 Breaking Out Animals
Published by Asian Culture Press LLC.
1942 Broadway, Suite 314C,
Boulder, CO 80302, United States.
Published in the United States of
America. First paperback edition
November 2022
ISBN 978-1-957144-63-4
Book by Jing Wu
Poems: Moonfell Xie, Jing Wu
Illustrations & design: Jing Wu
Translation: Jun Chen
Text editing: Joel Shephard

The awarding-winning artworks
in the book are granted Silver by
MUSE Creatie Awards 2022

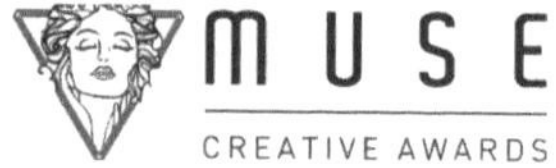

NFT of all artworks are available
to be purchased at opensea.io/
collection/the12animals

"The secret of change is to focus all of your energy, not on fighting the old, but on building the new."

- *Socrates*

Prologue   5

BOA #01-06   10
Mouse   12
Rabbit   14
Monkey   16
Goat   20
Ox   22
Horse   24
Tiger   26

BOA #07-12   28
Dragon   30
Dog   34
Snake   38
Rooster   40
Swine   42
Ending   44

Artworks   46

Prologue:

At the end of the 22nd century, scientists accidentally discovered a dimension that, with existing knowledge of physics, couldn't be explained. In this dimension, species are free from the shackles of time and space and are very different from anything seen in our plane of existence.

Twelve animals from the Zodiac have overturned their biological essences. Their exclusive energies

Twelve animals from the Zodiac have overturned their biological essences. Their exclusive energies from the future are awakened. Endowing great extradimensional powers that fabricate multiple units of discrete dimensions.

Each of the 12 animals dominates one space-time. The combined twelve parallel space-times have been named by scientists as the 12 BOA Universe.

In the twelve parallel space-times, animals are not restrained by matter. They are speedy wave-makers, free explorers, and masters over time. They can alter both the past and the future at will.

Now let's travel to the edge of
this universe, tunneling from our
dimension's brane and through
the brane of the BOA Universe, and
enter a brand-new reality together.

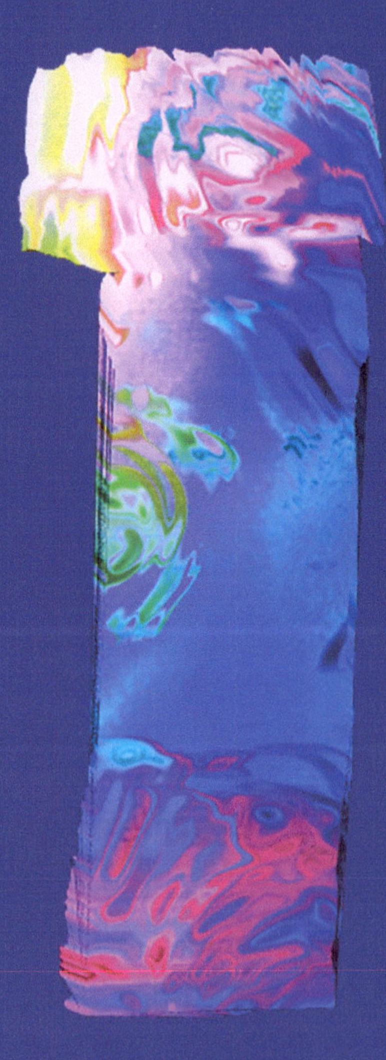

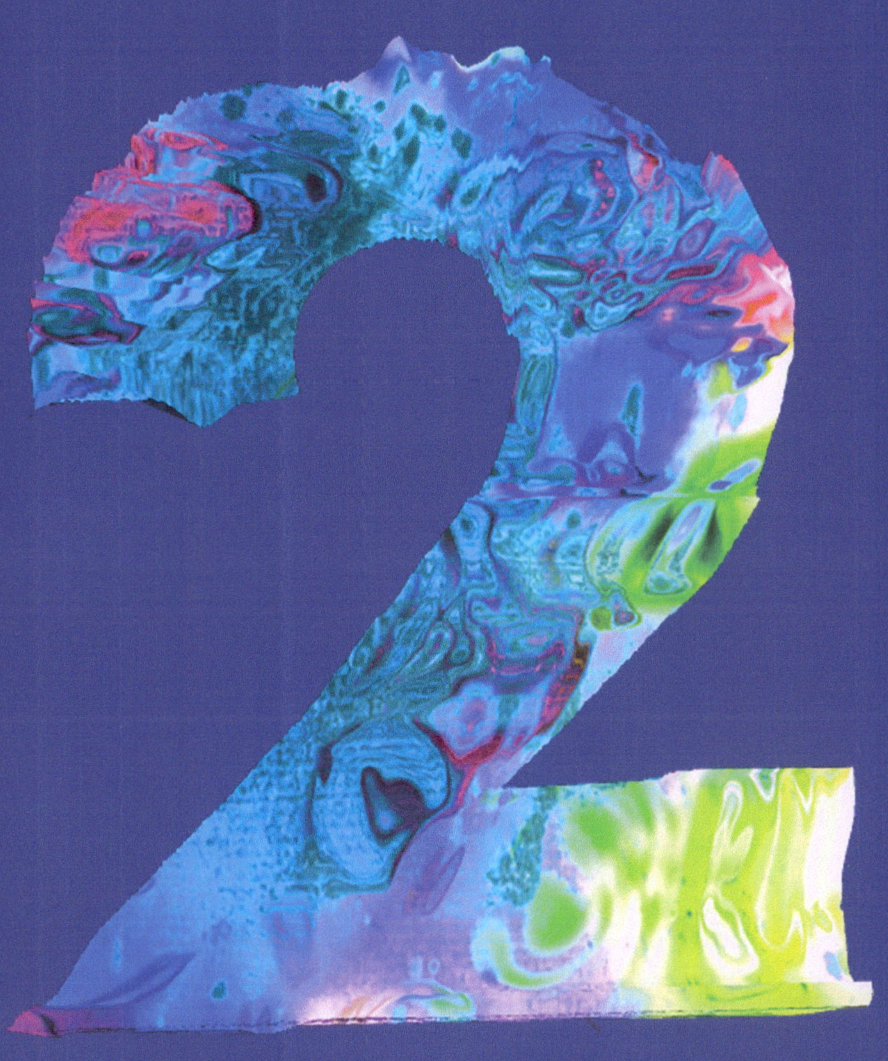

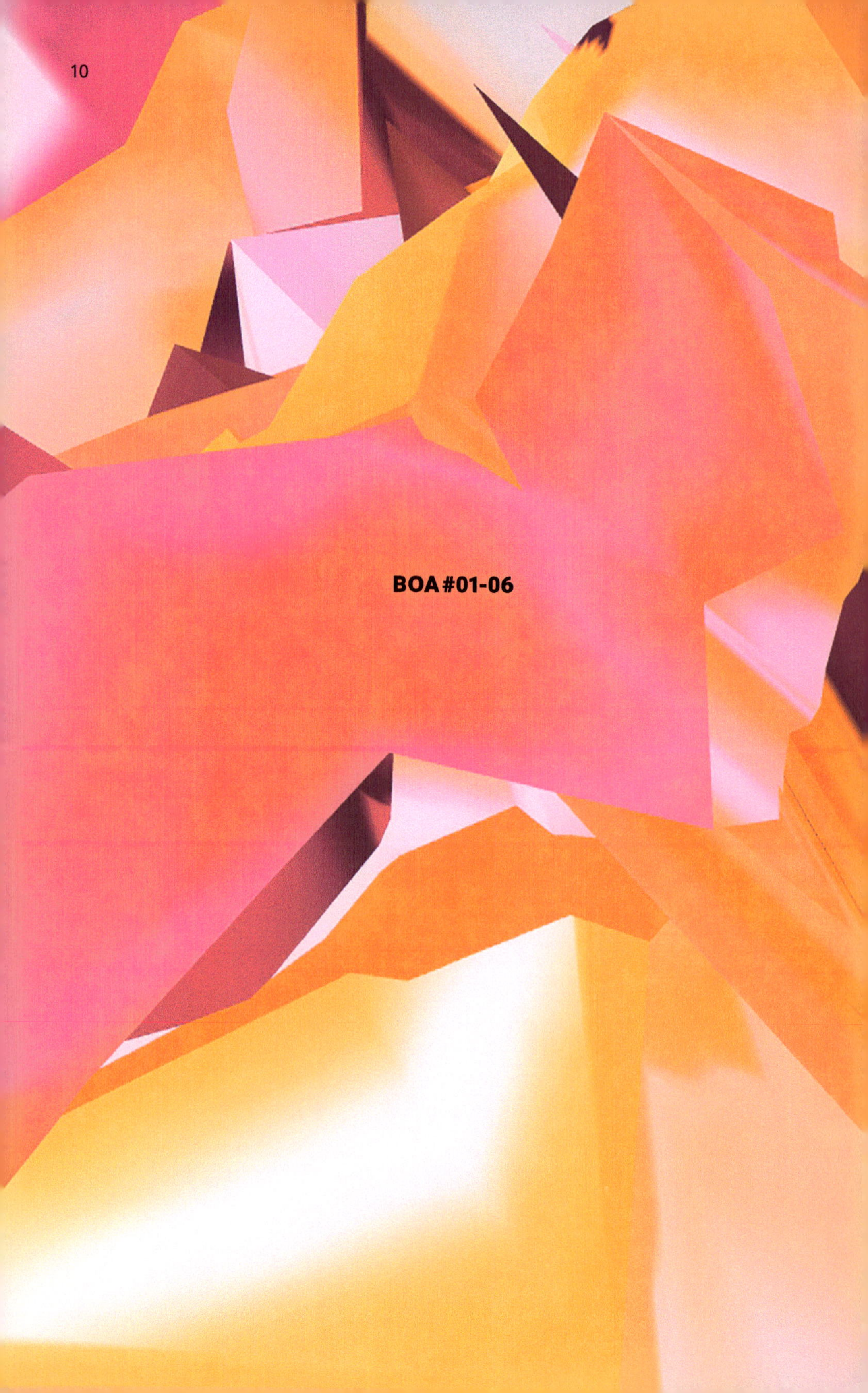
BOA #01-06

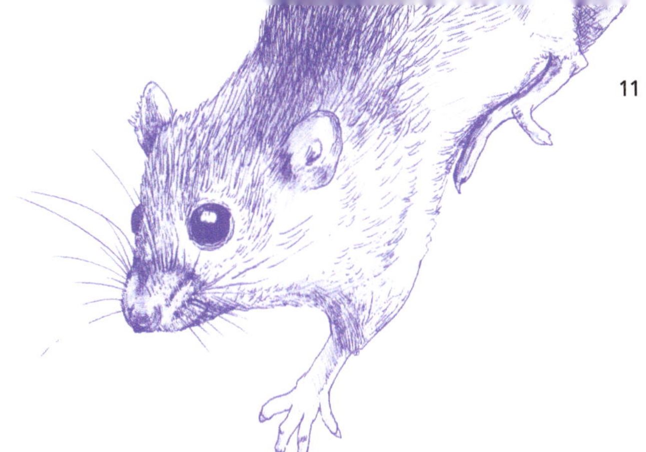

Let there be light.

At the birth of the BOA universe,
Mouse was the explorer of the dark
realm. It found the energy which
ignites the whole universe: Light.

Light awakens various dormant
elements gathering them up
continuously in the BOA universe to
form a unique energy field like the
event horizon of a black hole. With
the help of light, every animal starts
to evolve new superpowers.

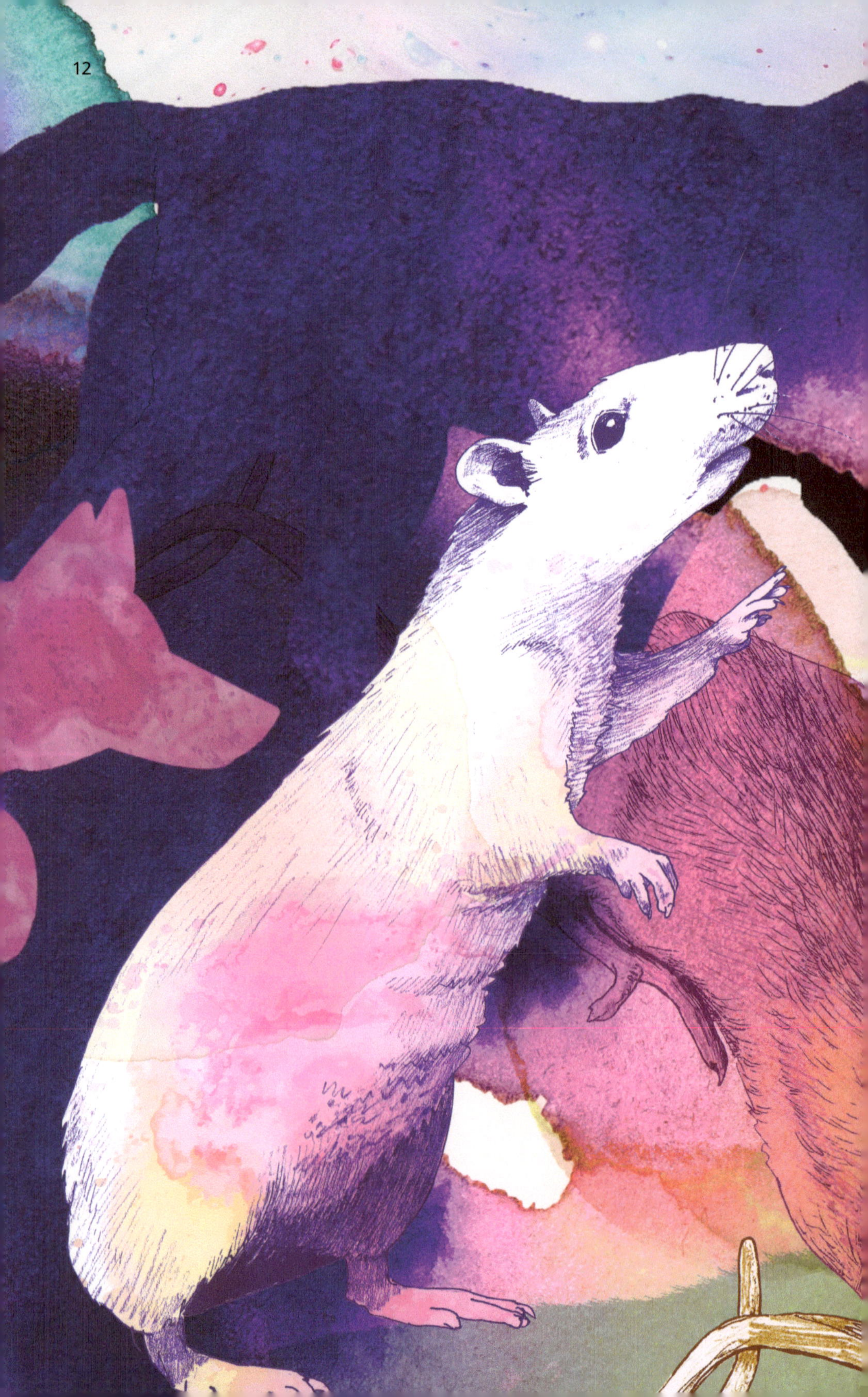

Light

In the dim ruins
comes the light.
Mouse's calling the animals
to see the show of light.

Light is the magician on the stage,
it conjures dancing shadows,
that form into blurs,
like clouds of a storm,
the stars and the sun
then changing into a brand-new world.

The interweaving light travels,
the broken corridors
are filled gradually by hypermatter.
The dim light, vaguely reveals
the black hole at the end,
reaching out its invisible hands,
dragging you into
the spacetime it creates.

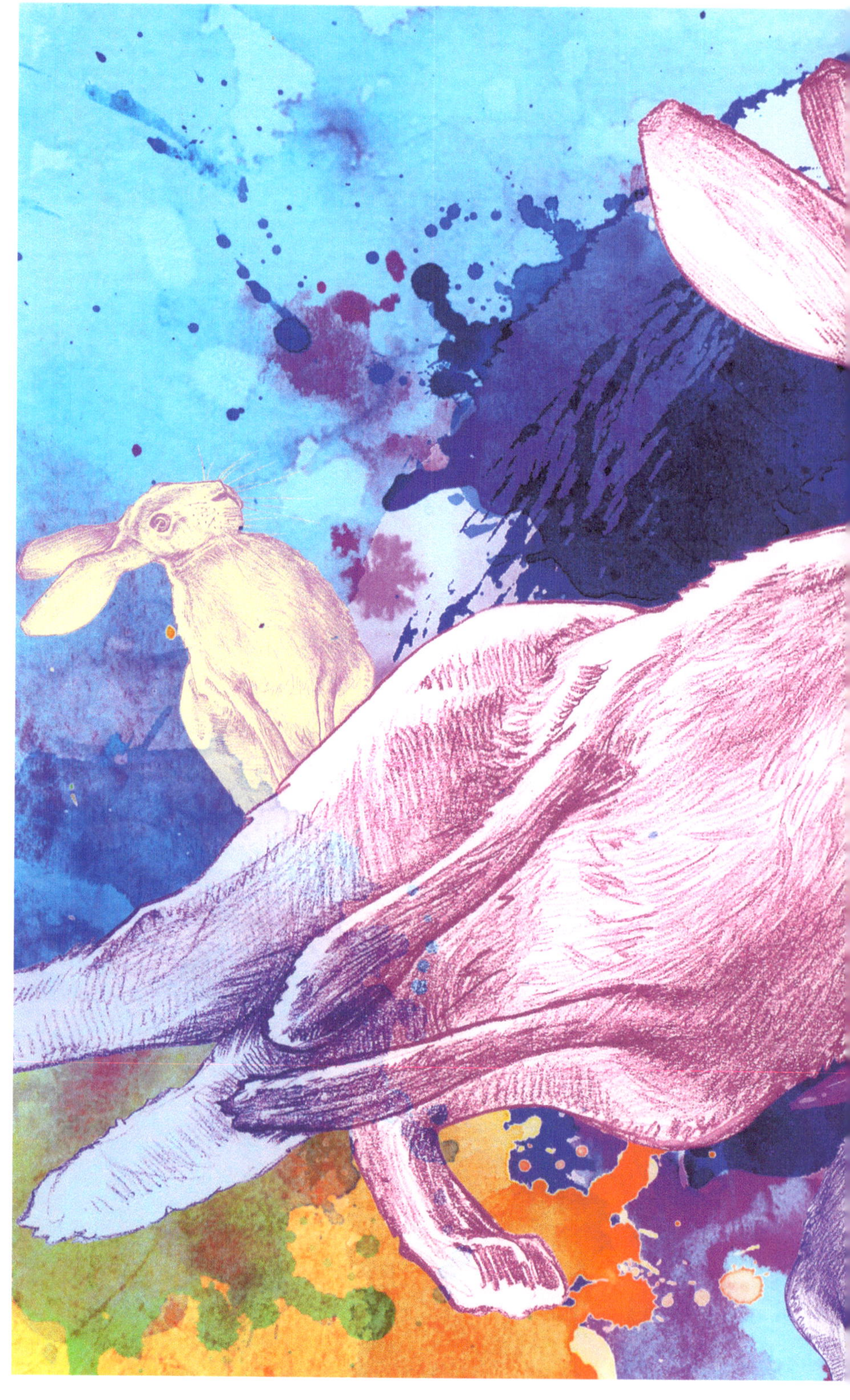

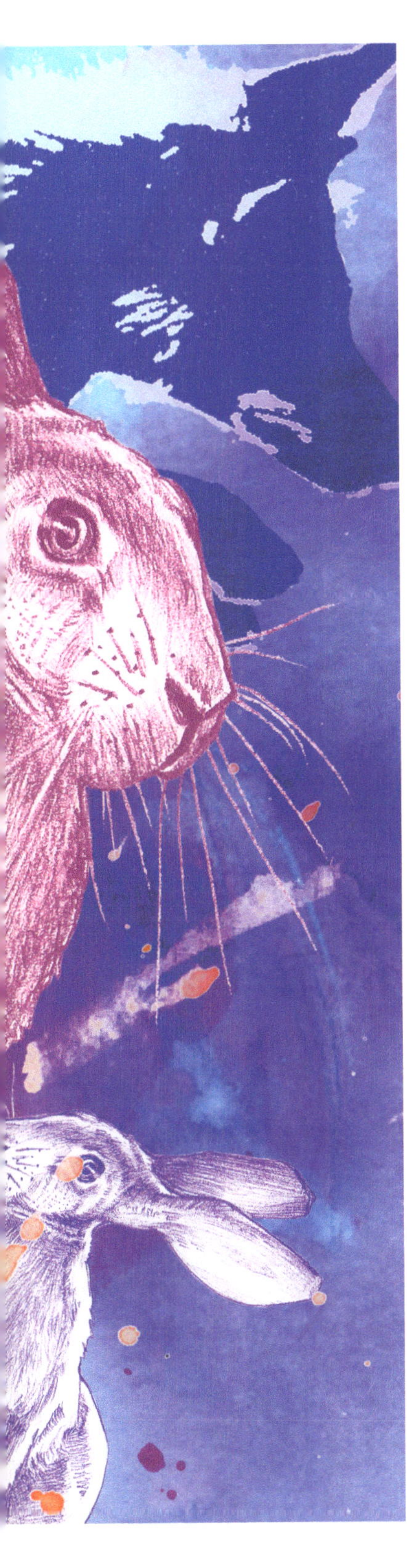

The cloth of the night

The night weaves a dark cloth
which rolls across the whole sky.
The cold wind makes the forests moan,
flinging needlelike droplets of rain,
and drives out those
that walk amongst the trees.

The wolfpacks are howling,
waking Rabbit.
Rabbit uses feathers as armor
and branches as spears.
It drives the wolfpacks to charge forward
to the top of the mountains.
They tear the dark cloth apart,
stars pour out into the sky and shimmer,
which guards the animals' migration to
new homes.

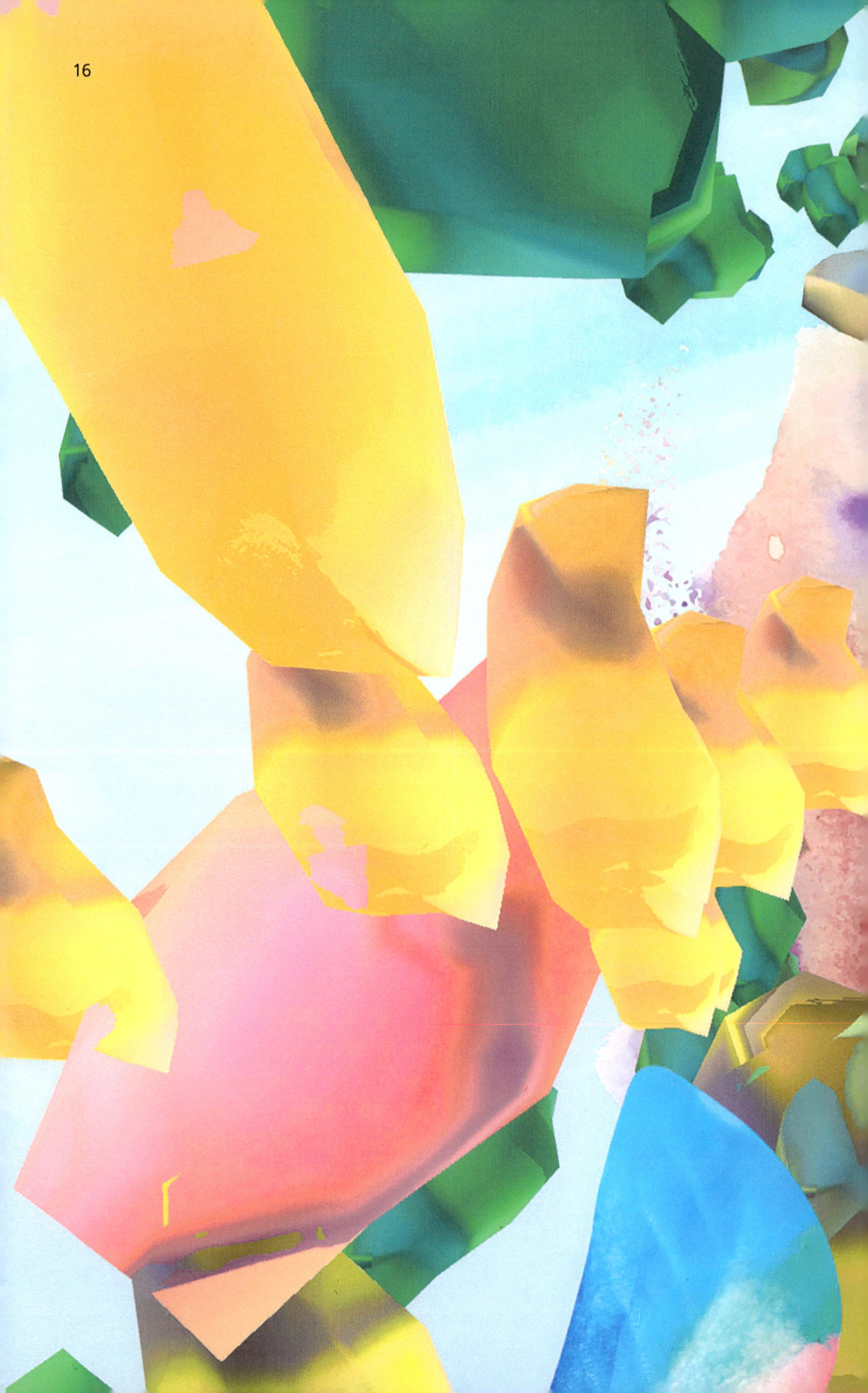

Mind Imposer

The vast ocean of stars
is compressed into the brain.
The whole universe is contained
in a tiny little nutlet.

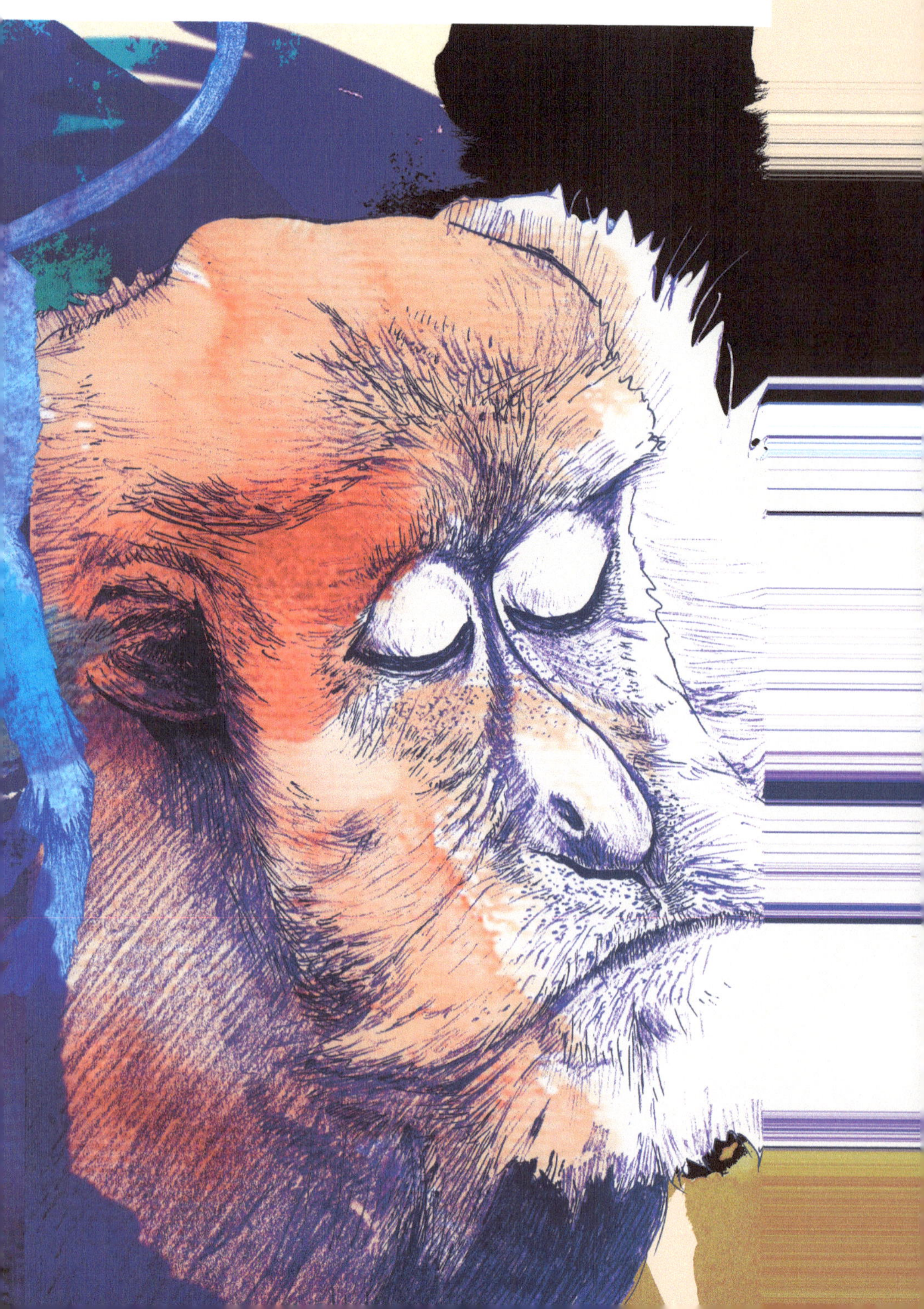

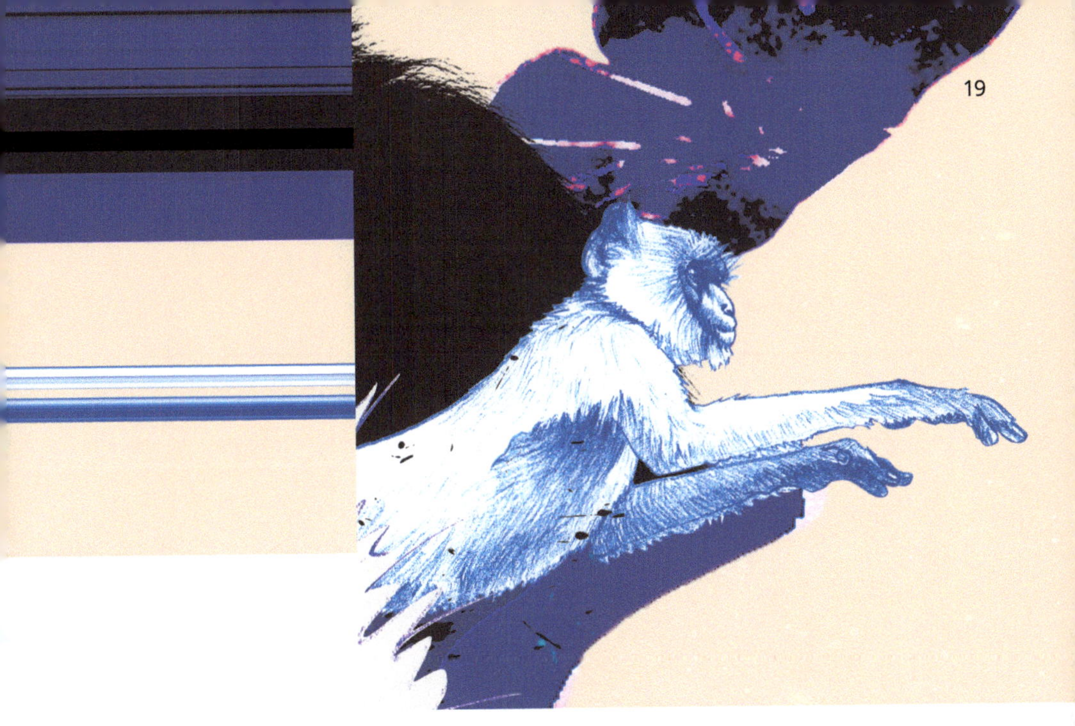

Time is moving

The brain is the best weapon of all.
Thought has the power
to move time and space.

When Monkey thinks,
the whole world reverses
and rotates upside down,
like the hands of God,
it controls the will of others.

The dislocated sun rises in the sky,
it's the ghost in the machine,
which duplicates infinitely,
and reflects the same faces,
deceiving your vision.

Goat, is the creator of this place.
It disrupts the old order and
dislocates everything,
leaving no room for revolt.
After the new order takes its place,
no one can tell the way it used to be.

Cyber Sun

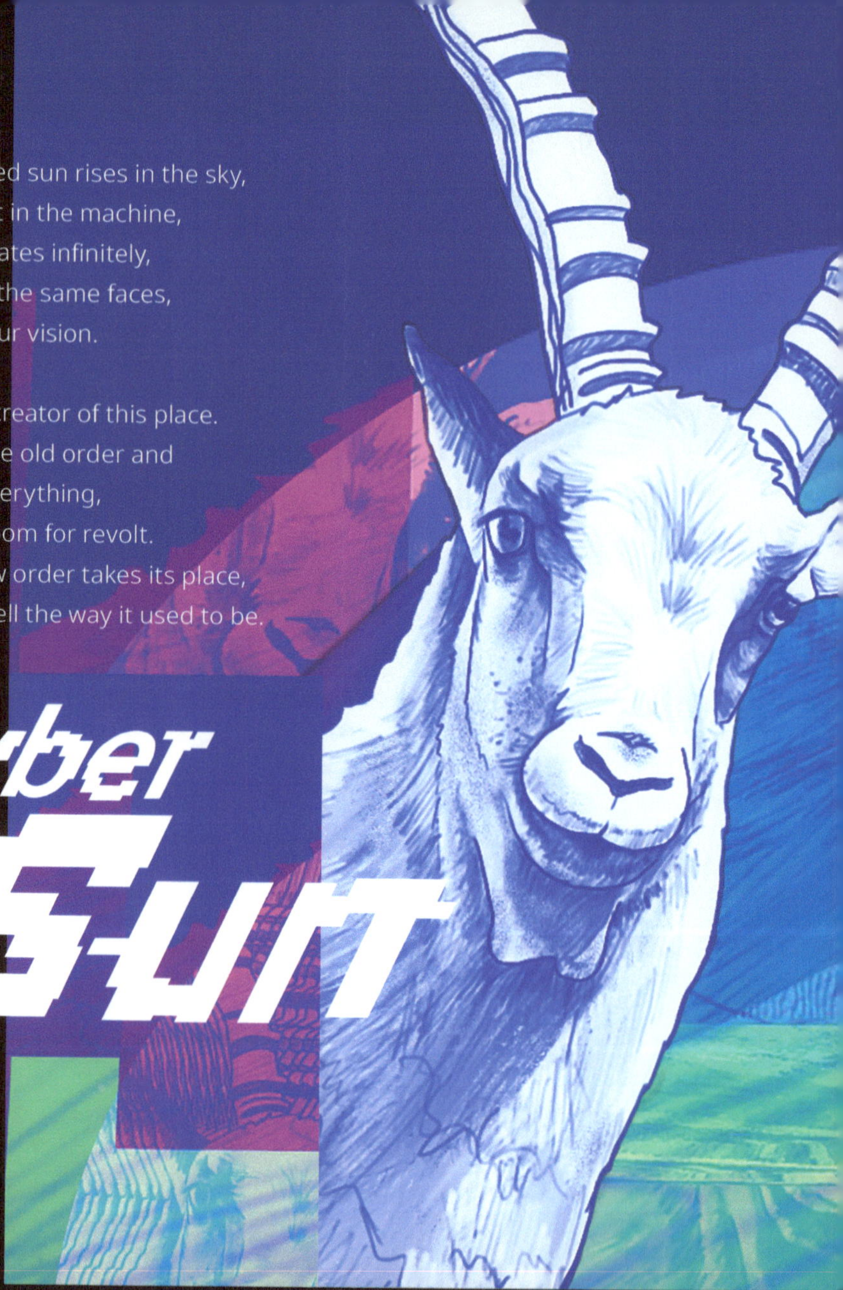

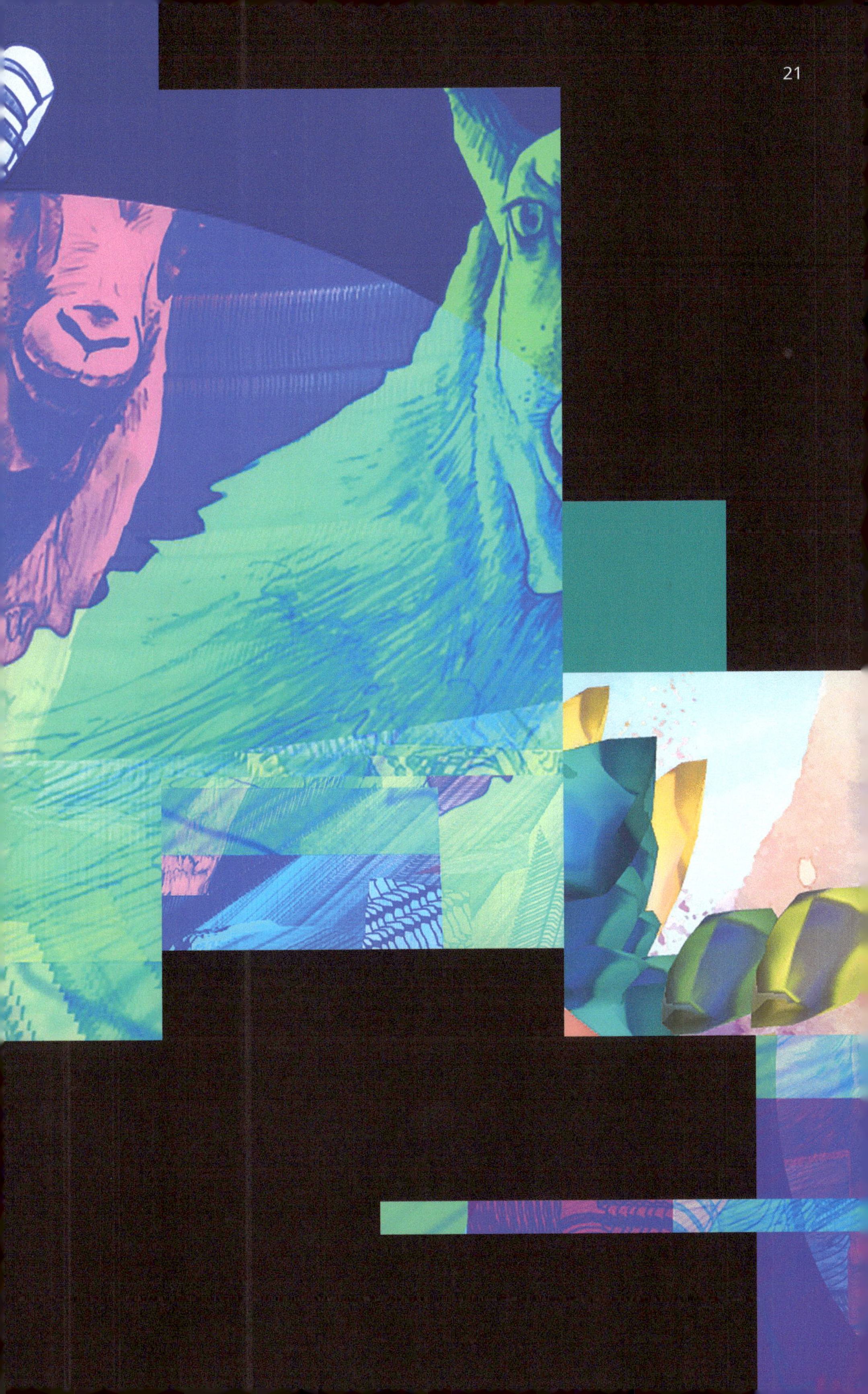

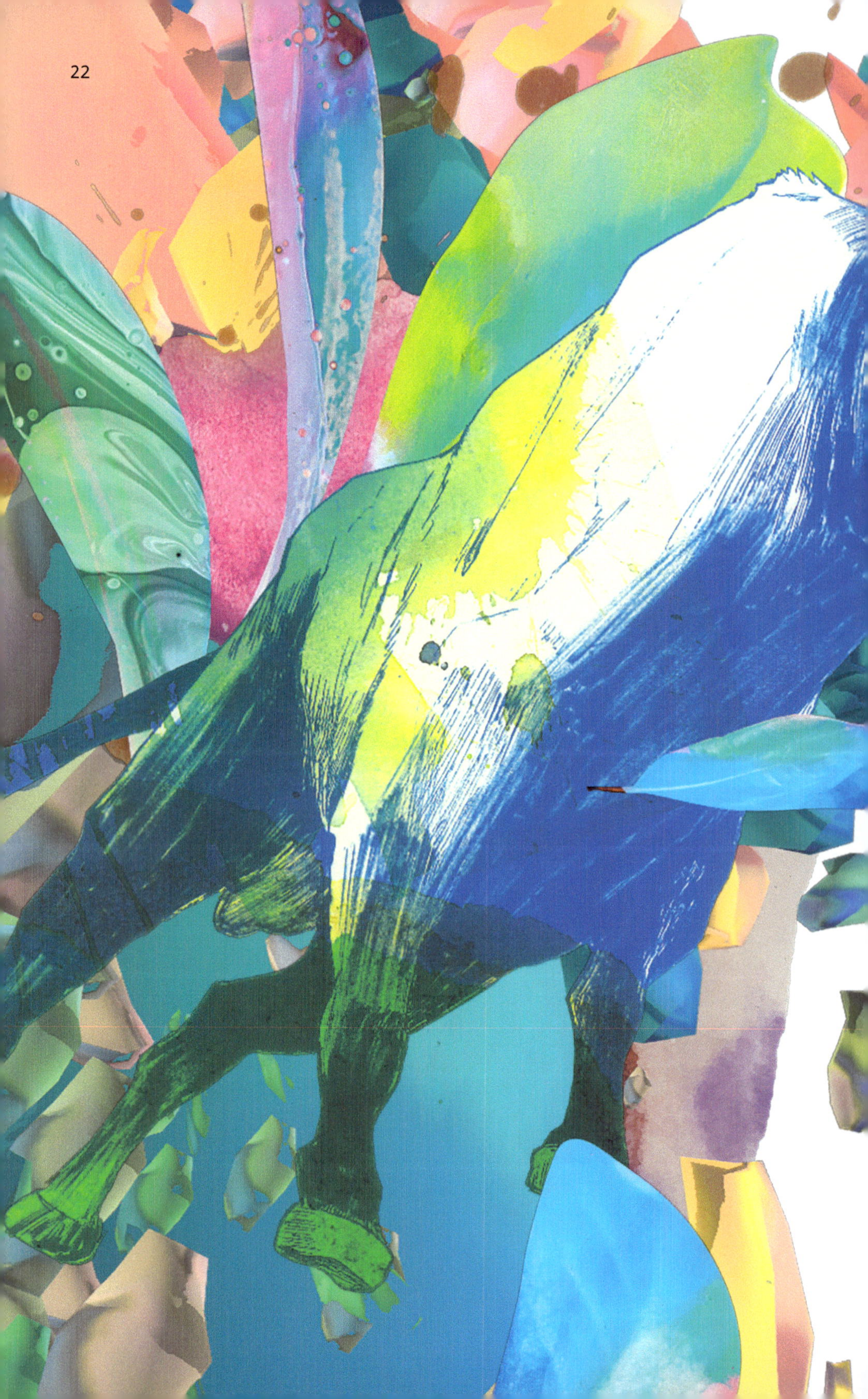

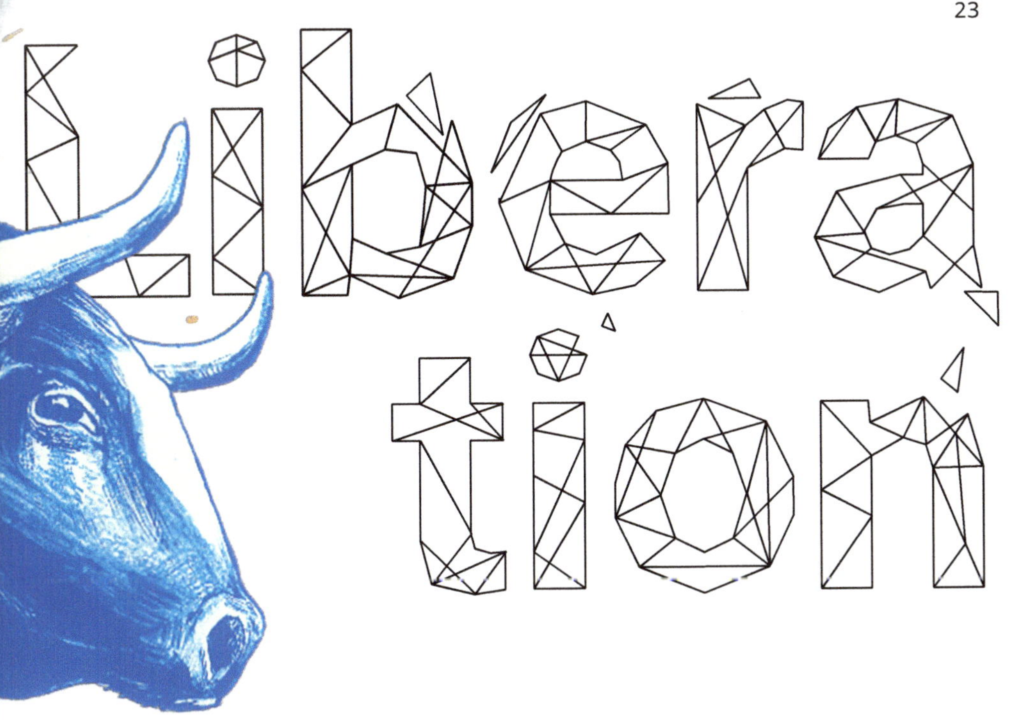

A spring breeze blows the rally horn,
Ox the warrior like a weed,
is about to break out of the earth.

The leaf veins weave into armor,
and the sap becomes courage passing into cells
until its horns become unbreakable.
Ox forces through barrier after barrier.
When the final rally horn blasts,
the warrior bursts into the forbidden place
outside the old spacetime.

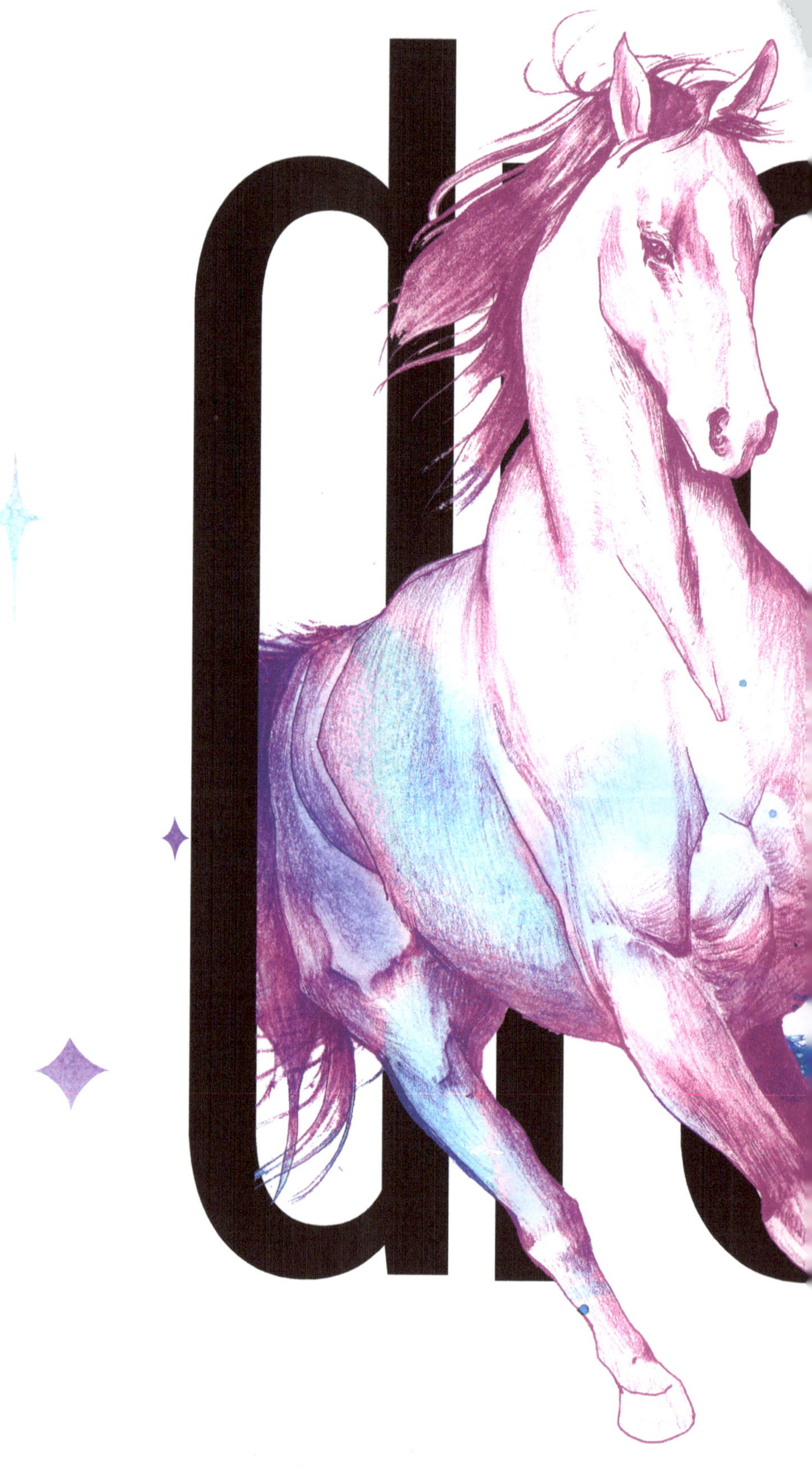

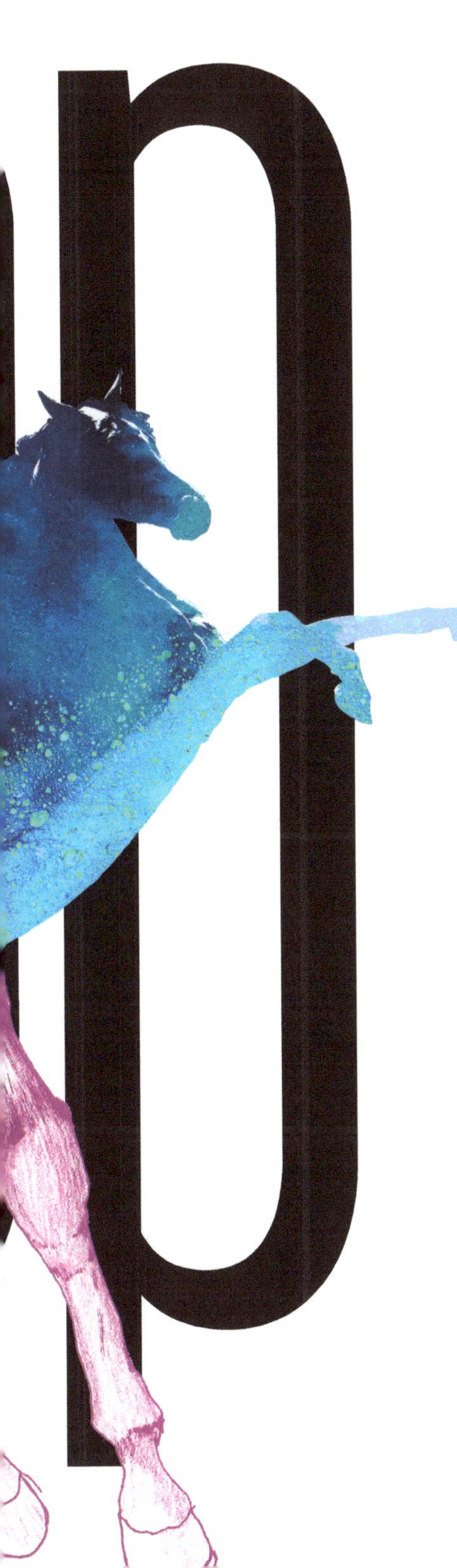

The star
wanderer

This is an adventure full of
romance and wonder,
the destination of which
is the ocean of stars.
Horse, the wanderer, sets sail,
giant sharks are the boats
amongst the stars,
and icebergs are the lighthouses
that lead the way through hazy
purple clouds and mists.

The horizon connects,
and it becomes the bridge underfoot,
so that it can step on the stars and
run all the way.

Wave Making

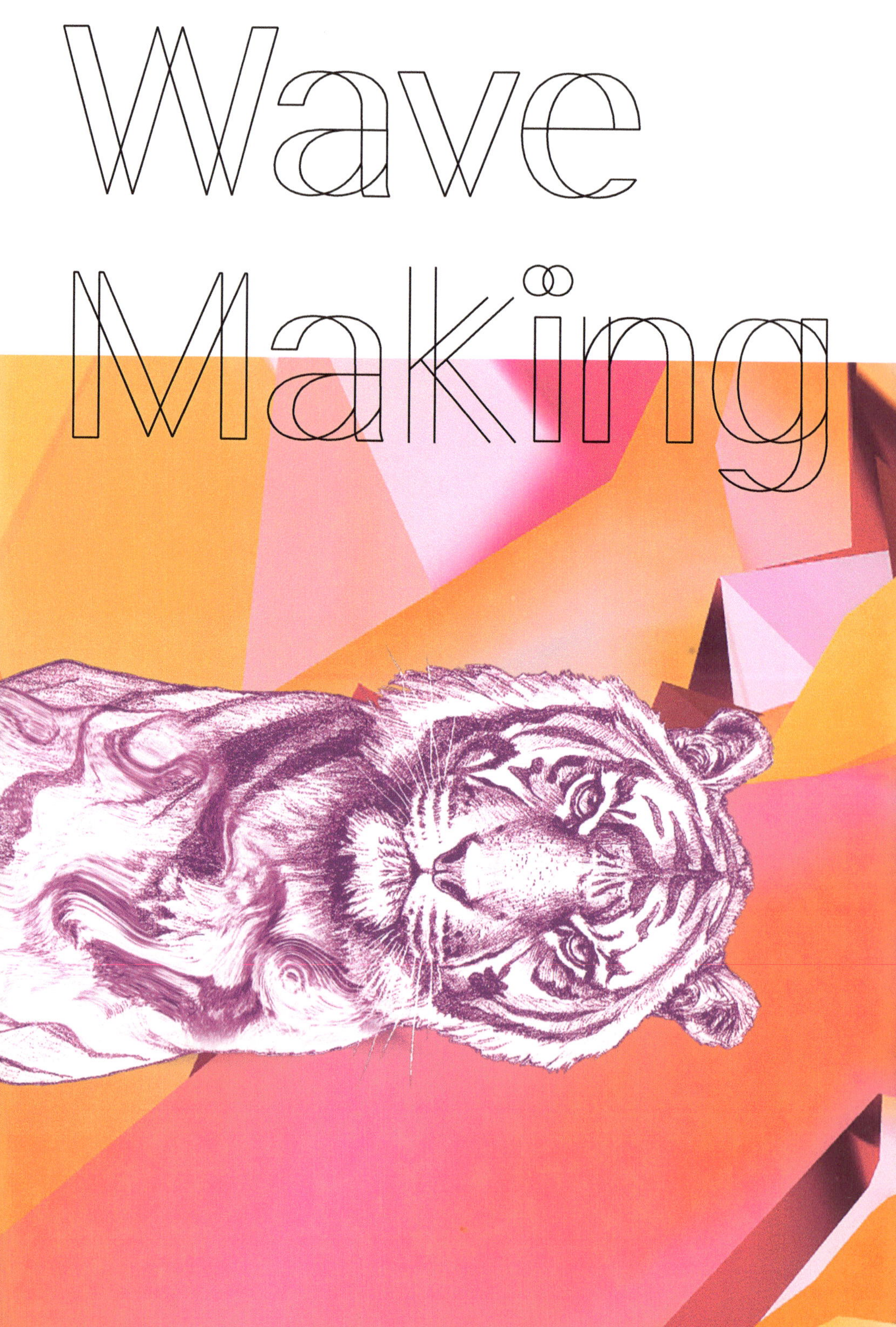

Tiger, the wave-maker, is the explorer
who breaks the dimensional wall,
marking footprints on the
land unknown,
draws the first map by measuring the
length with both feet.

Tiger is the lord of virtual space-time,
its steps are like spoondrift,
and the sea waves like vigorous beasts,
chasing and lurching forward,
The waves behind drive on those before,
fighting to be the first to trespass upon
the unknown land.

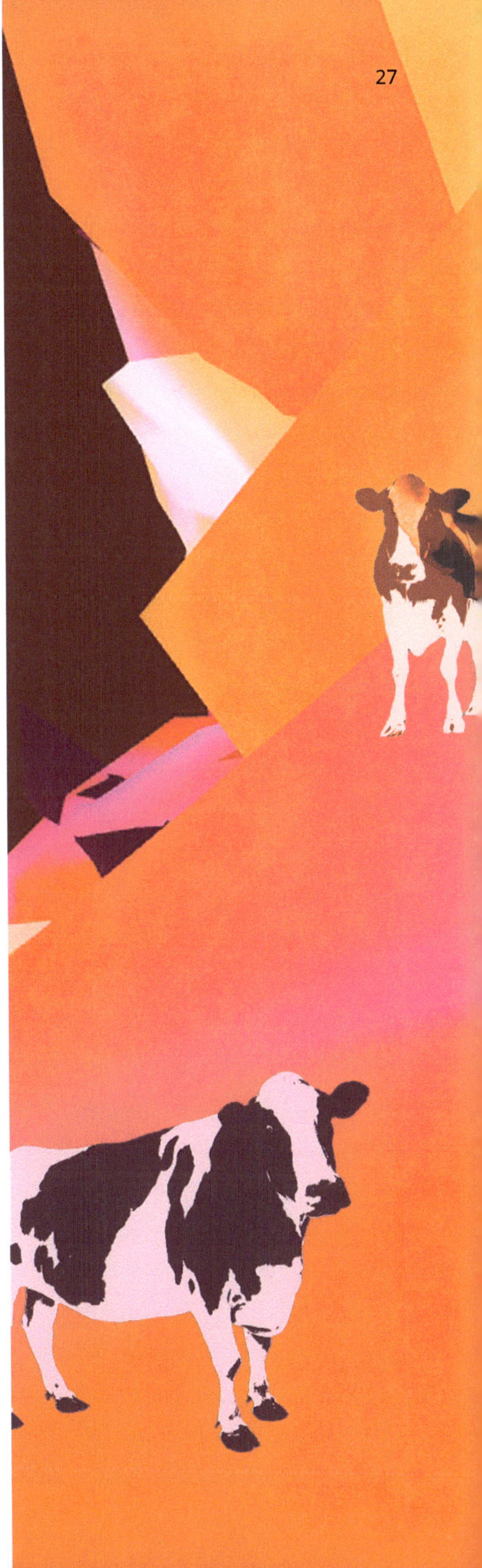

BOA #07-12

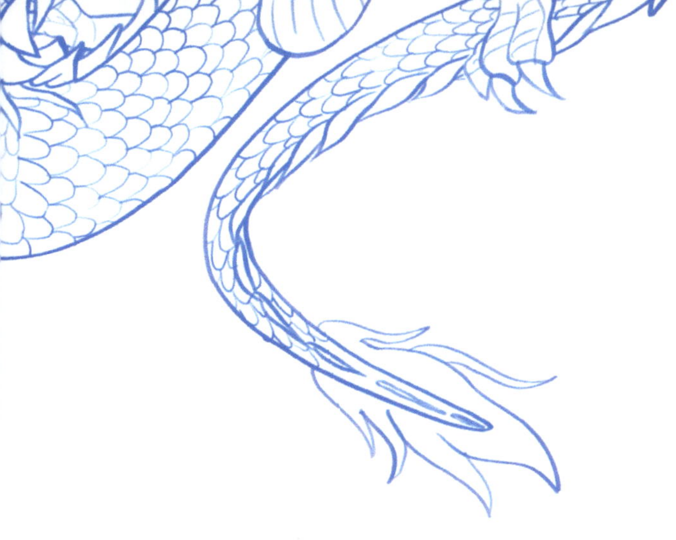

The Storm is coming.

During the birth of the BOA Universe comes an unprecedented massive "storm." It brings the dark realm back, almost devastating the entire new order, and every species faces the danger of being devoured.

Dragon, the creature that enjoys the most incredible vitality, uses its scales to defend against the storm, making it the first survivor. It restrains the tempest firmly in its dimension.

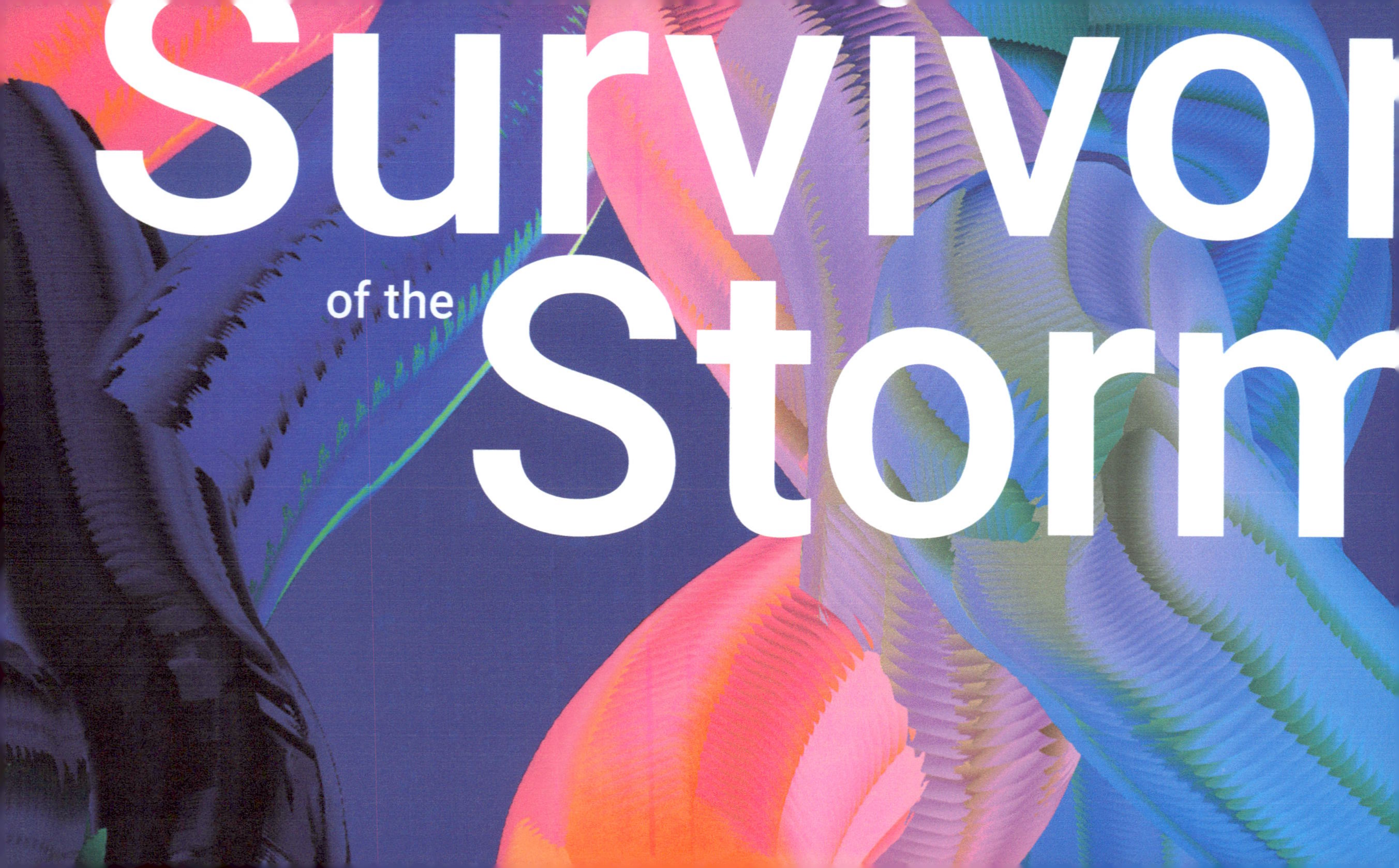
Survivor
of the
Storm

The dark clouds strike,
the storm suddenly breaks,
Dragon dives into the eye of the storm,
and fights against the tempest.

The storm carries the dark realm,
entwining the vines like tangled flames,
climbs on its body,
and burns its scales.
The melted scales flow down gently,
like colored ribbons
winding around its body softly.

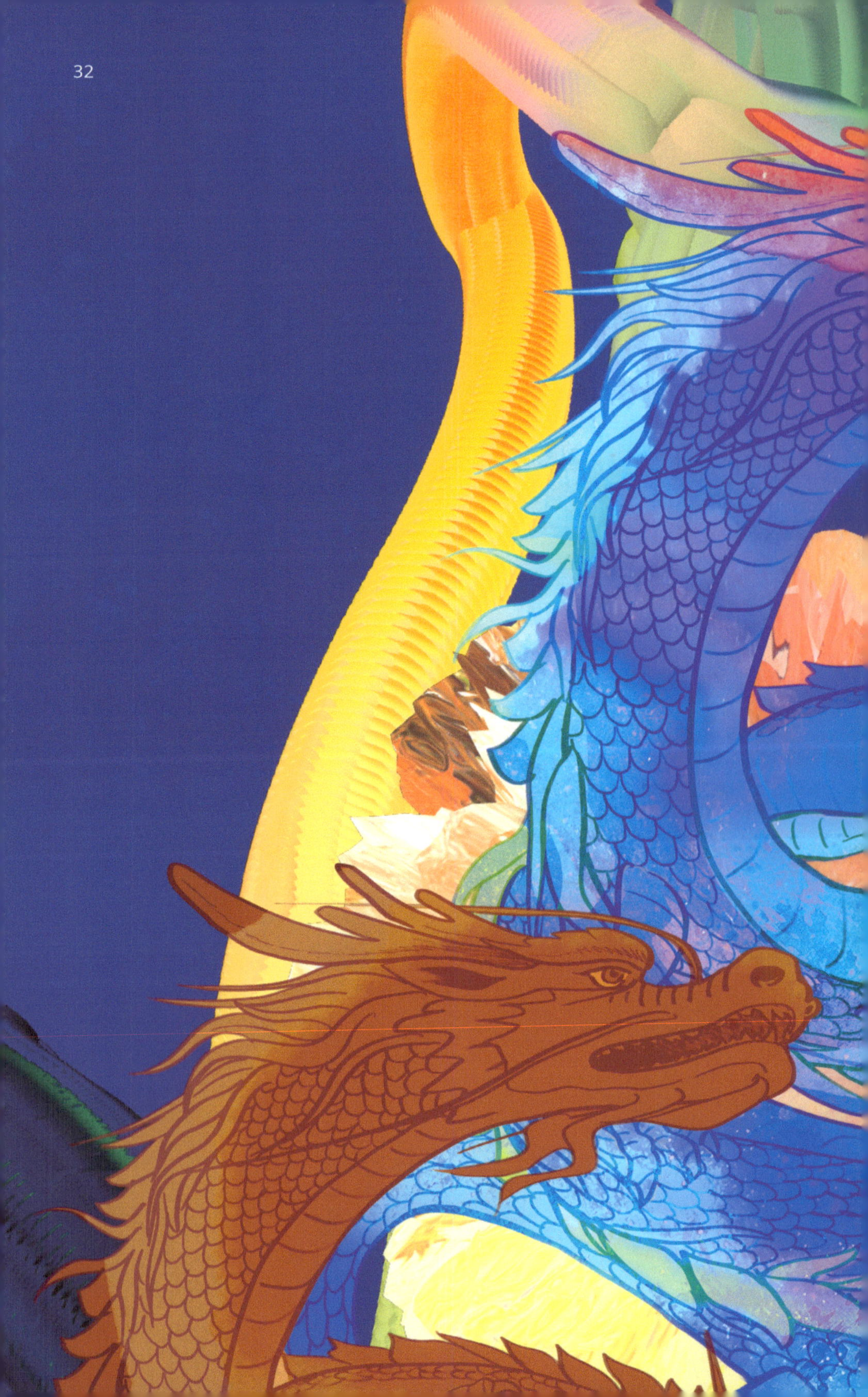

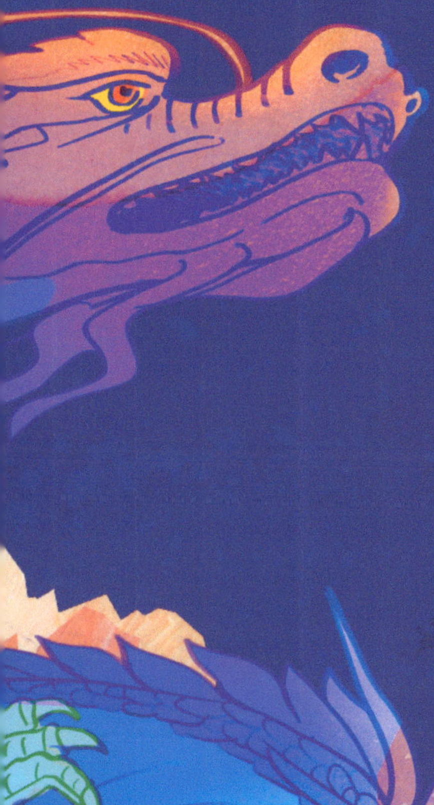

The cloud and mist
can't make it submit.
As if whispering an invitation
to play together,
Dragon curls up by the clouds,
and enjoys the storm.

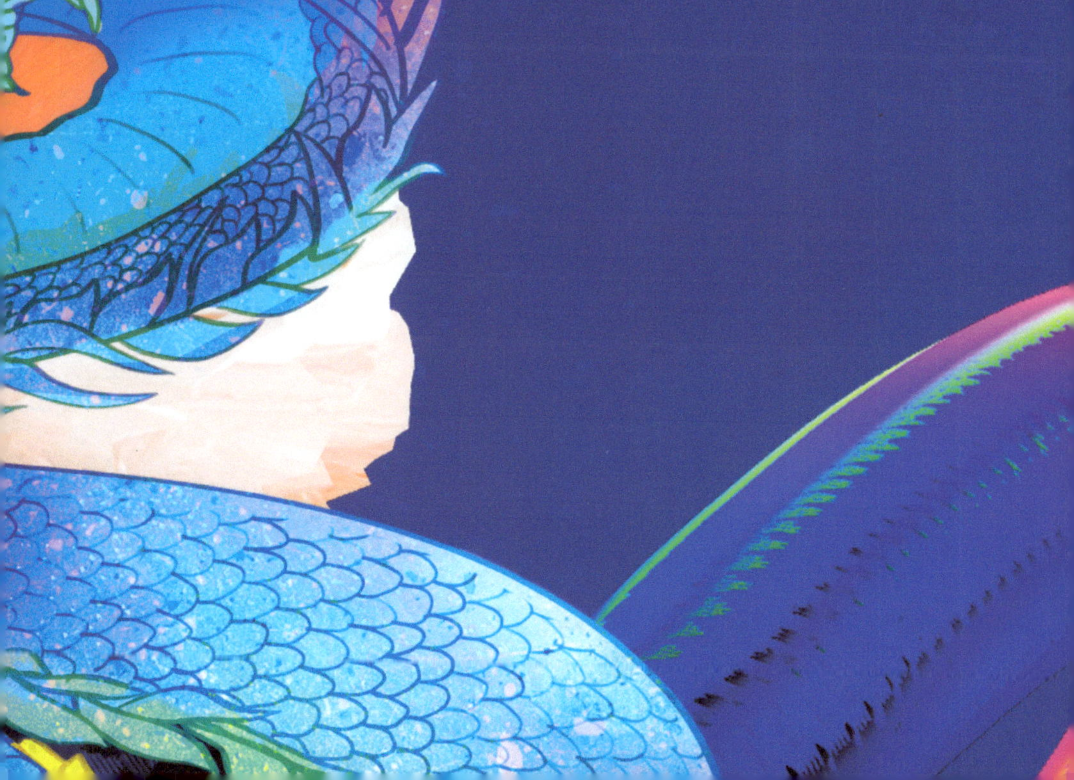

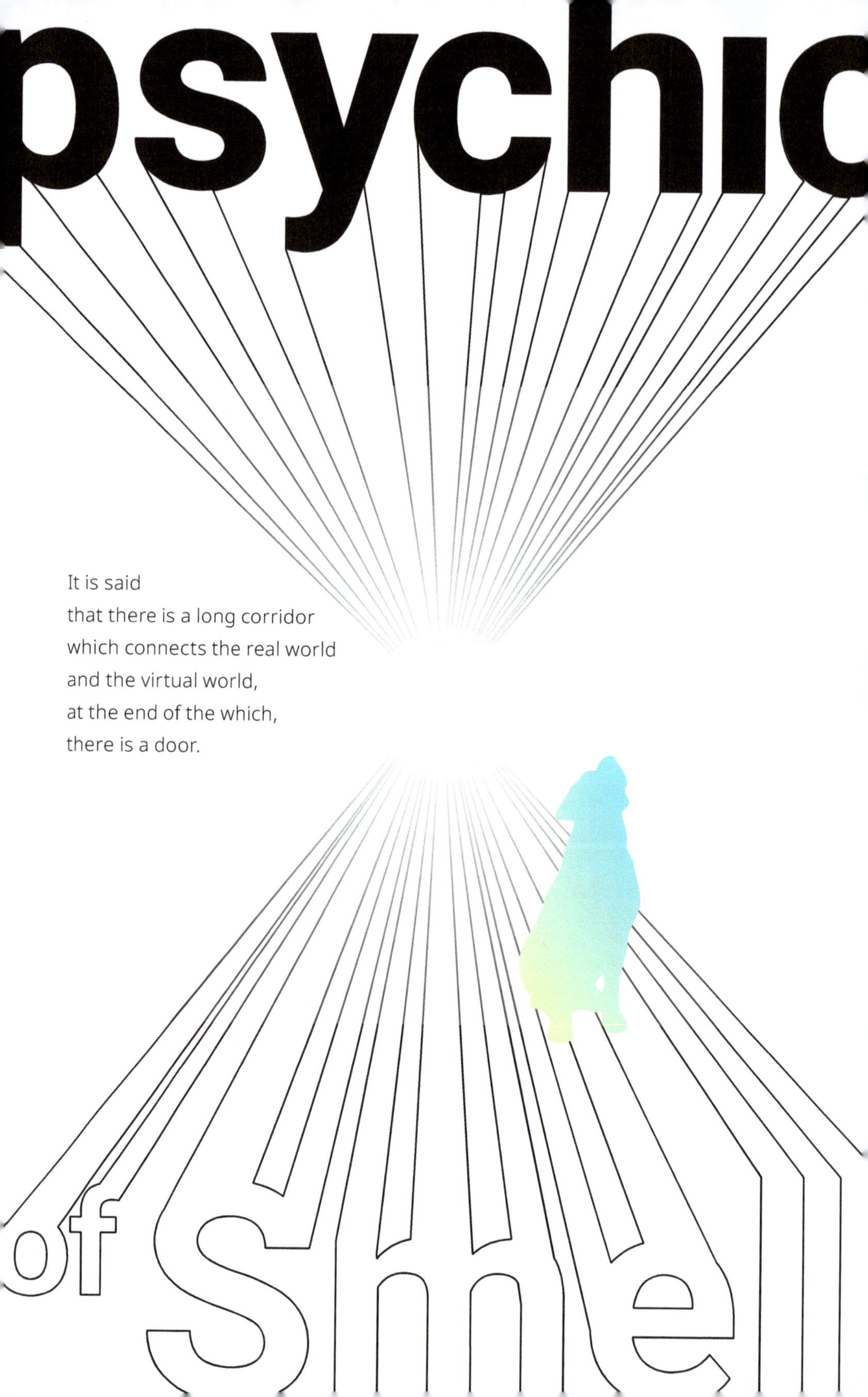

psychic
It is said
that there is a long corridor
which connects the real world
and the virtual world,
at the end of the which,
there is a door.
of Shnell

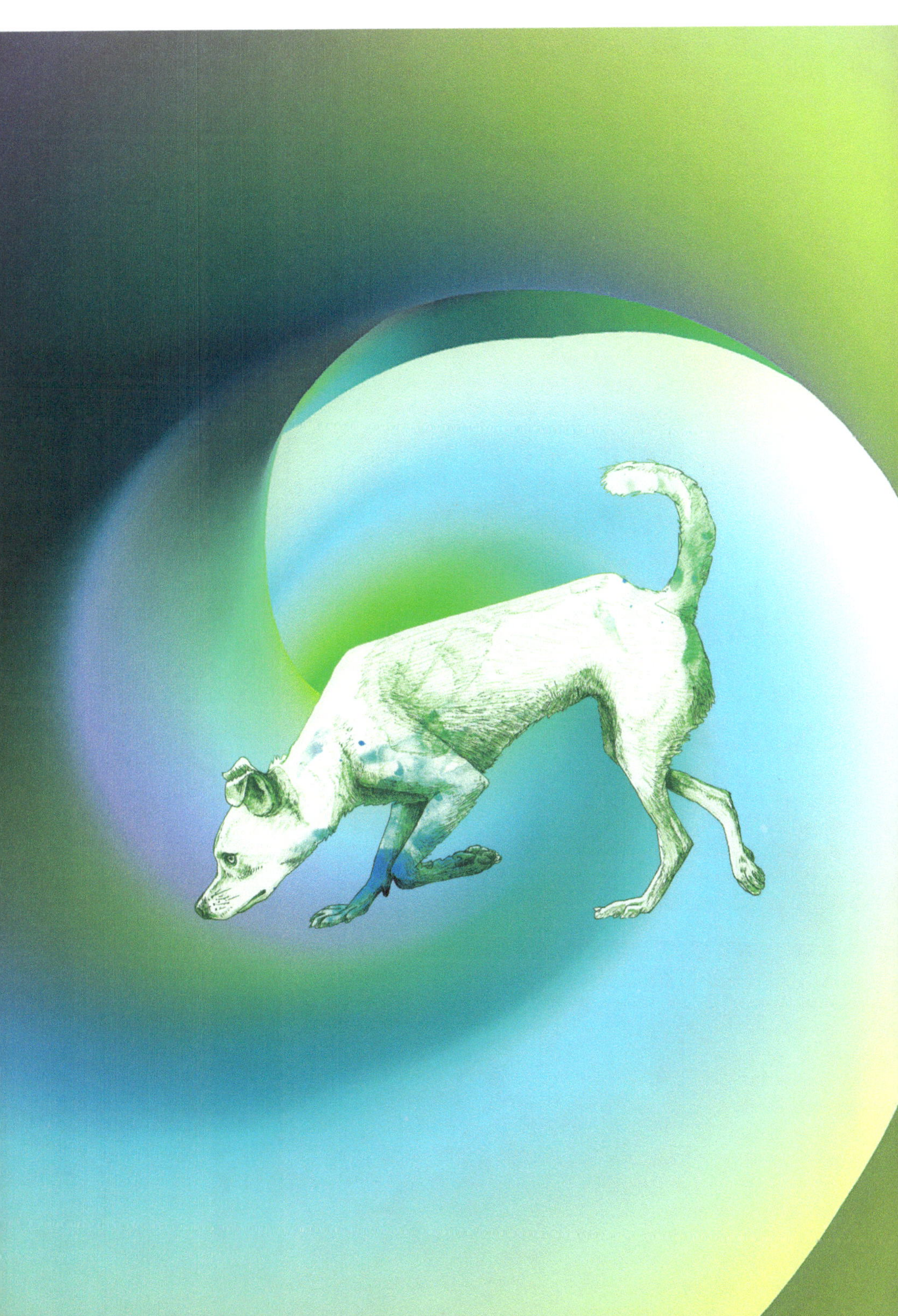

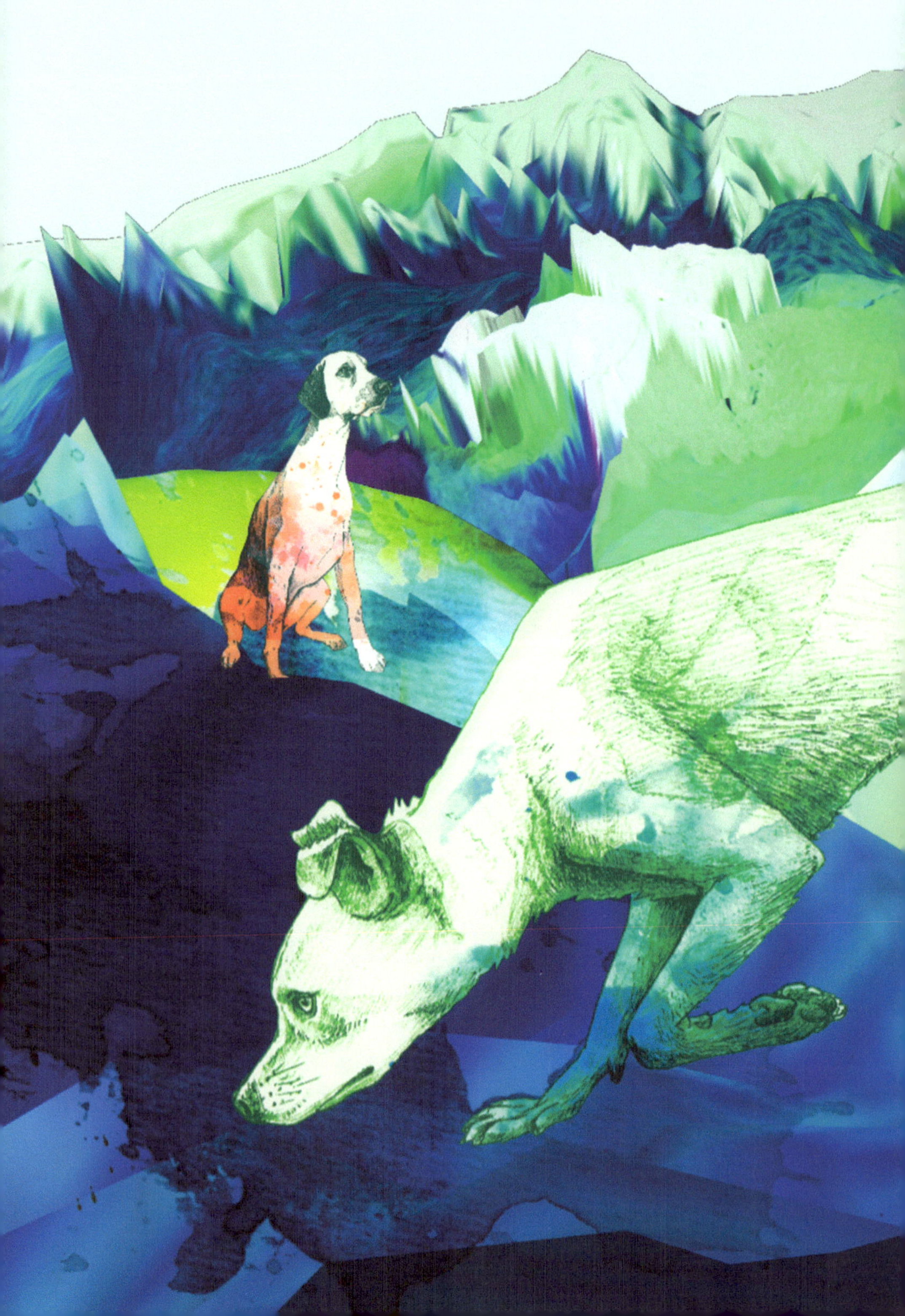

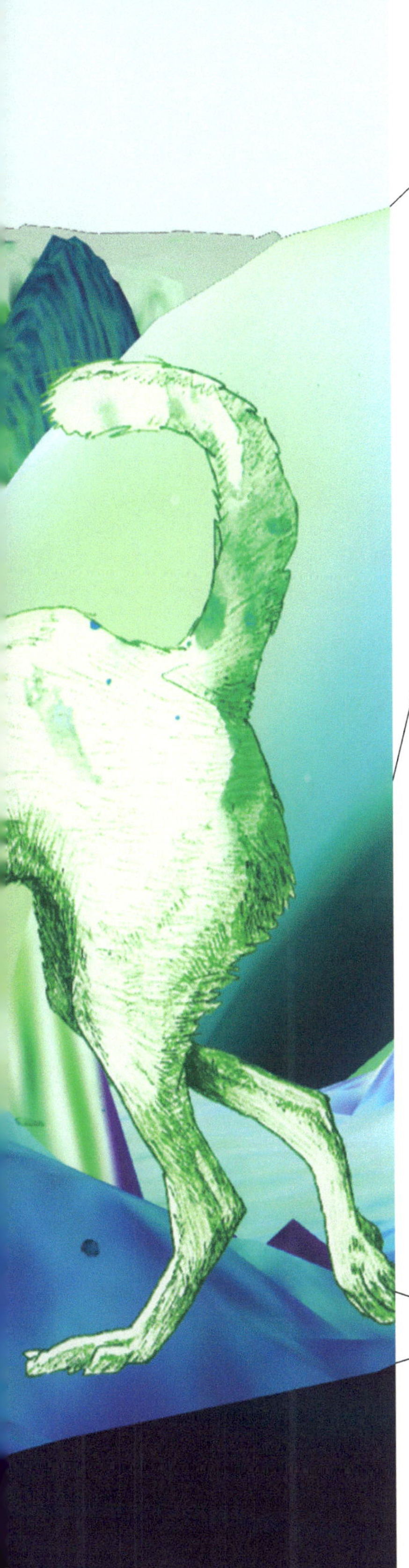

An amber-like dark realm
covers the door,
Blocking the future like a curse.
Only Dog can feel it,
as it possesses special powers.

It can use its nose to search for every
clue from the future.
The seal is broken, and
the static universe starts to operate.
The door to the unknown world
is smashed open.

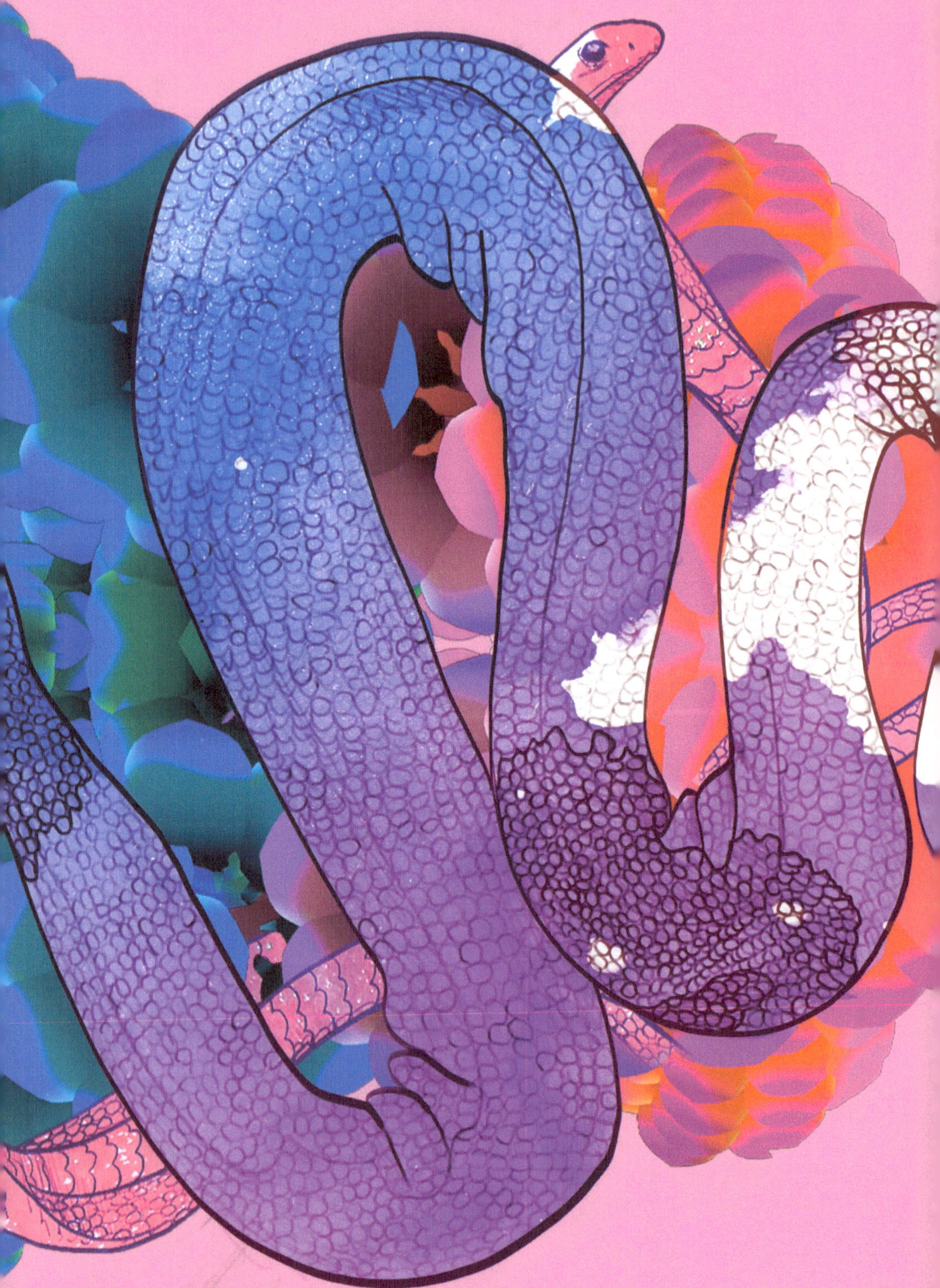

In Disguise

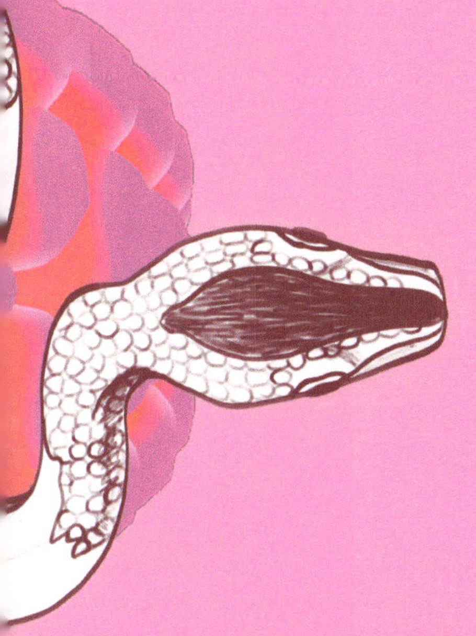

The garden in the spring
is an inspiration of colors.
The darkness of the soil,
the purple of the berries,
the pink shades of wildflowers,
are all drawn and melt into Snake's skin.

The bright colors,
and the flowers blooming on its scales,
roll across its body tight,
making it invisible.

The secret working of nature,
and the perfect camouflage,
quietly hiding within the chaos,
until it sneaks into the extraordinary
blooming space-time.

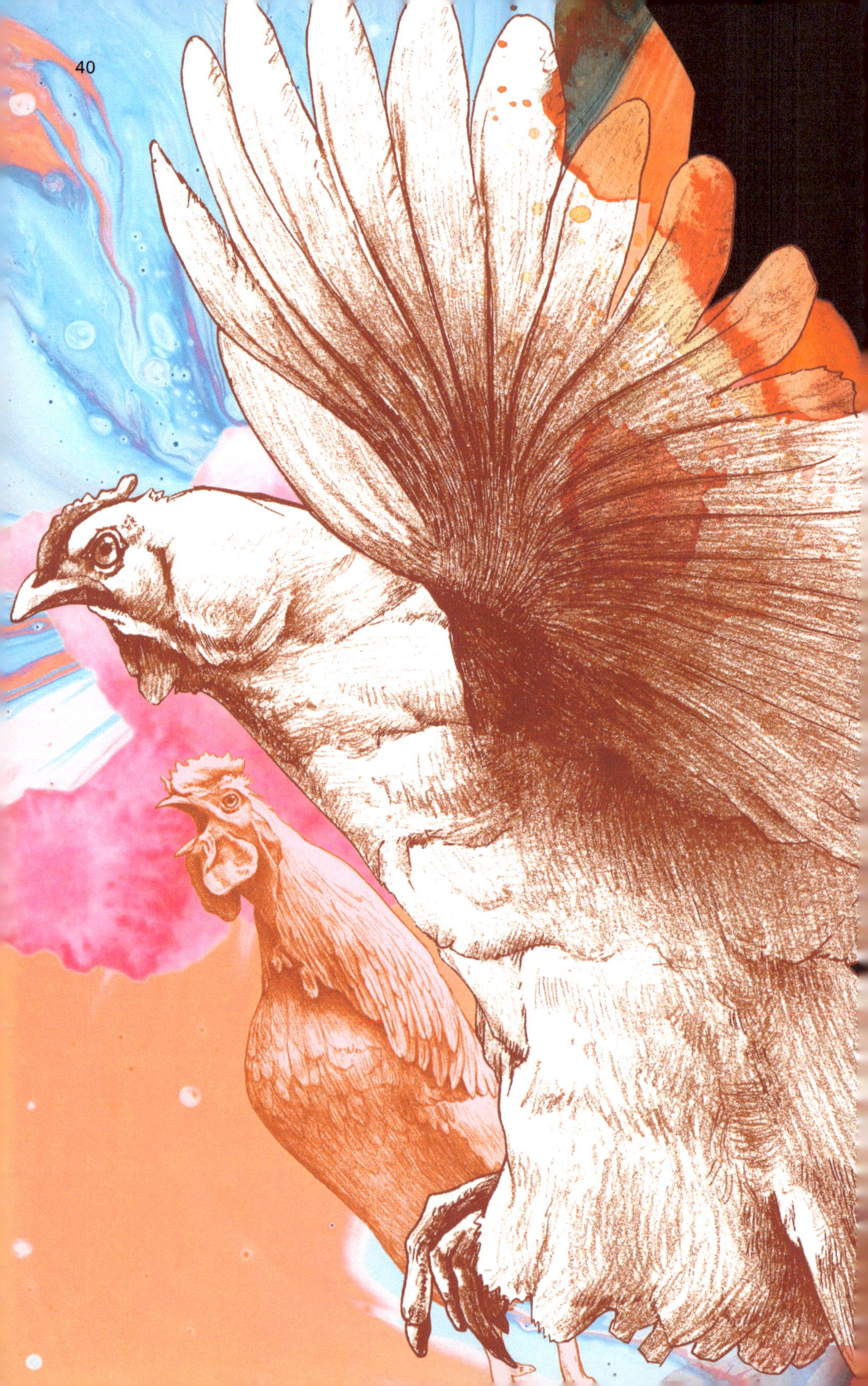

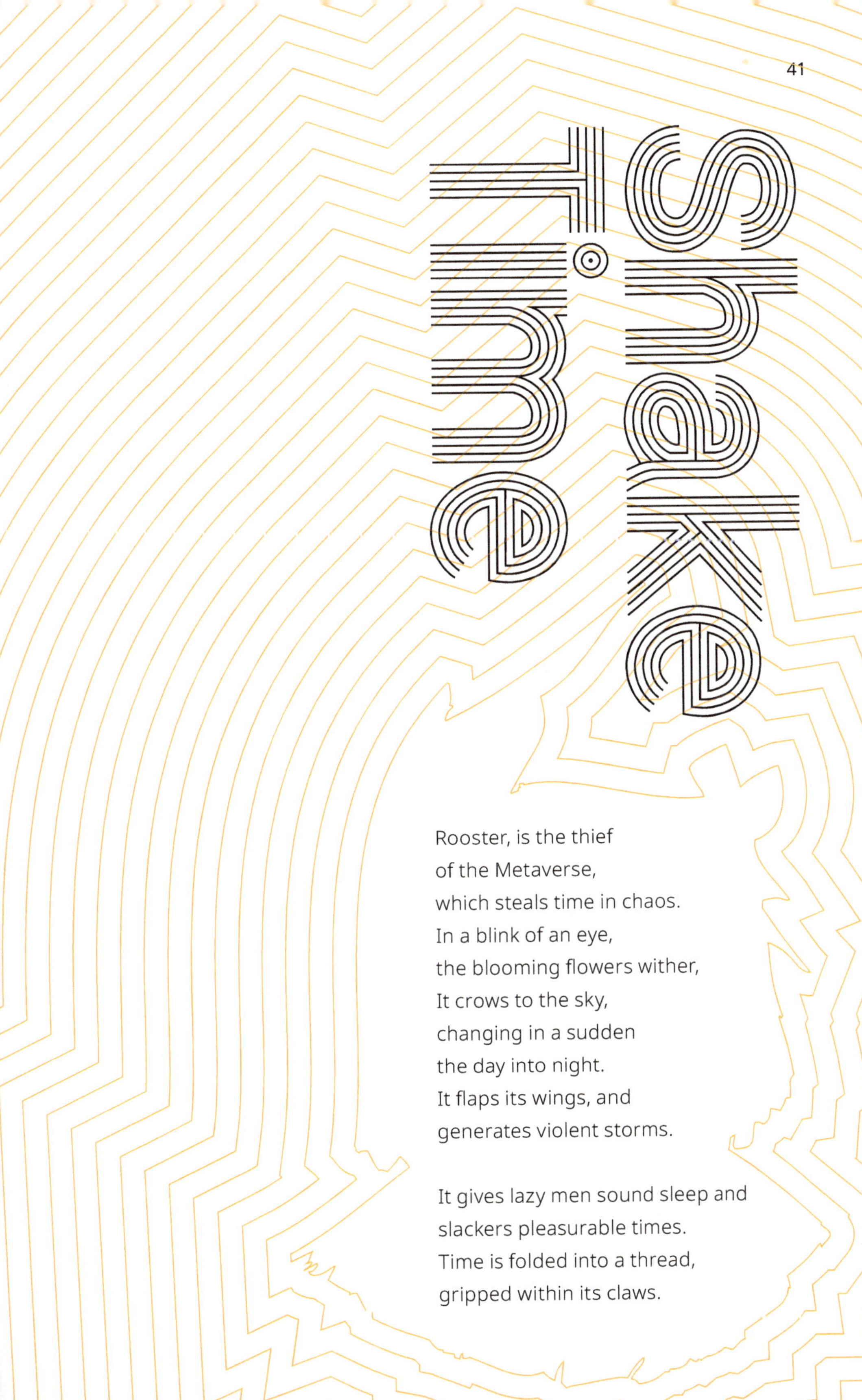

Rooster, is the thief
of the Metaverse,
which steals time in chaos.
In a blink of an eye,
the blooming flowers wither,
It crows to the sky,
changing in a sudden
the day into night.
It flaps its wings, and
generates violent storms.

It gives lazy men sound sleep and
slackers pleasurable times.
Time is folded into a thread,
gripped within its claws.

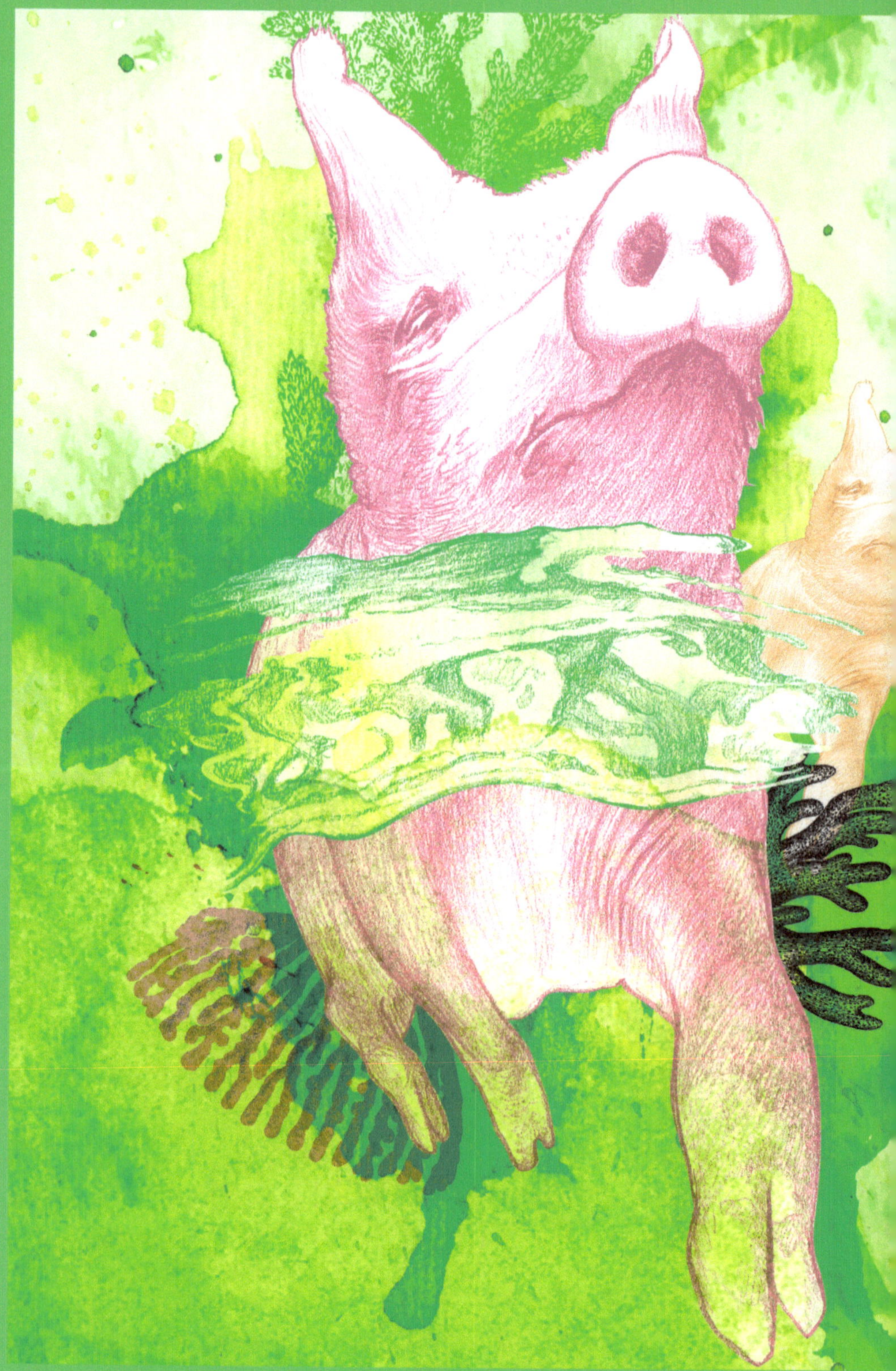

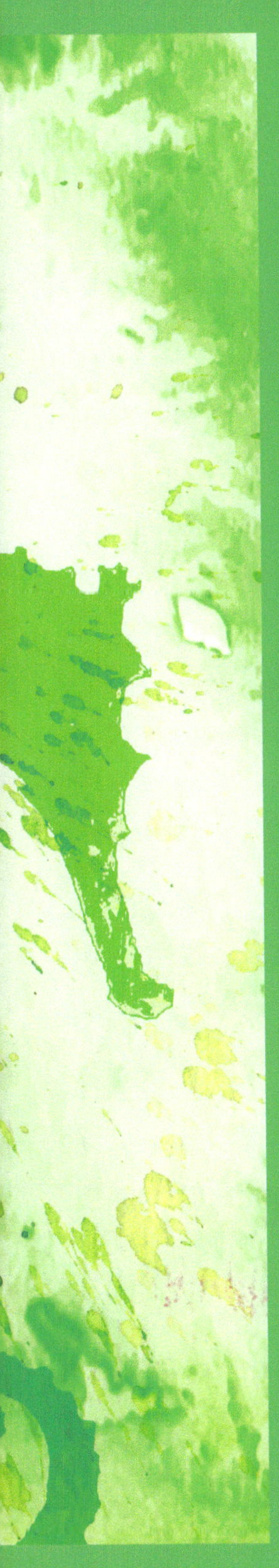

Master of Waters

If you were born in the water,
the water is air.
Bubbles are its companies,
a pair of wings are gifted by the stream,
so it can happily fly in the deep sea,
The seaweeds oscillate coloured
ribbons for celebration,
the green sea horses dance around.

The gorgeous corals are transparent
or flickering with light, like fireworks
at the bottom of the ocean.
May it ride the wind and waves,
may it become the master of the sea.

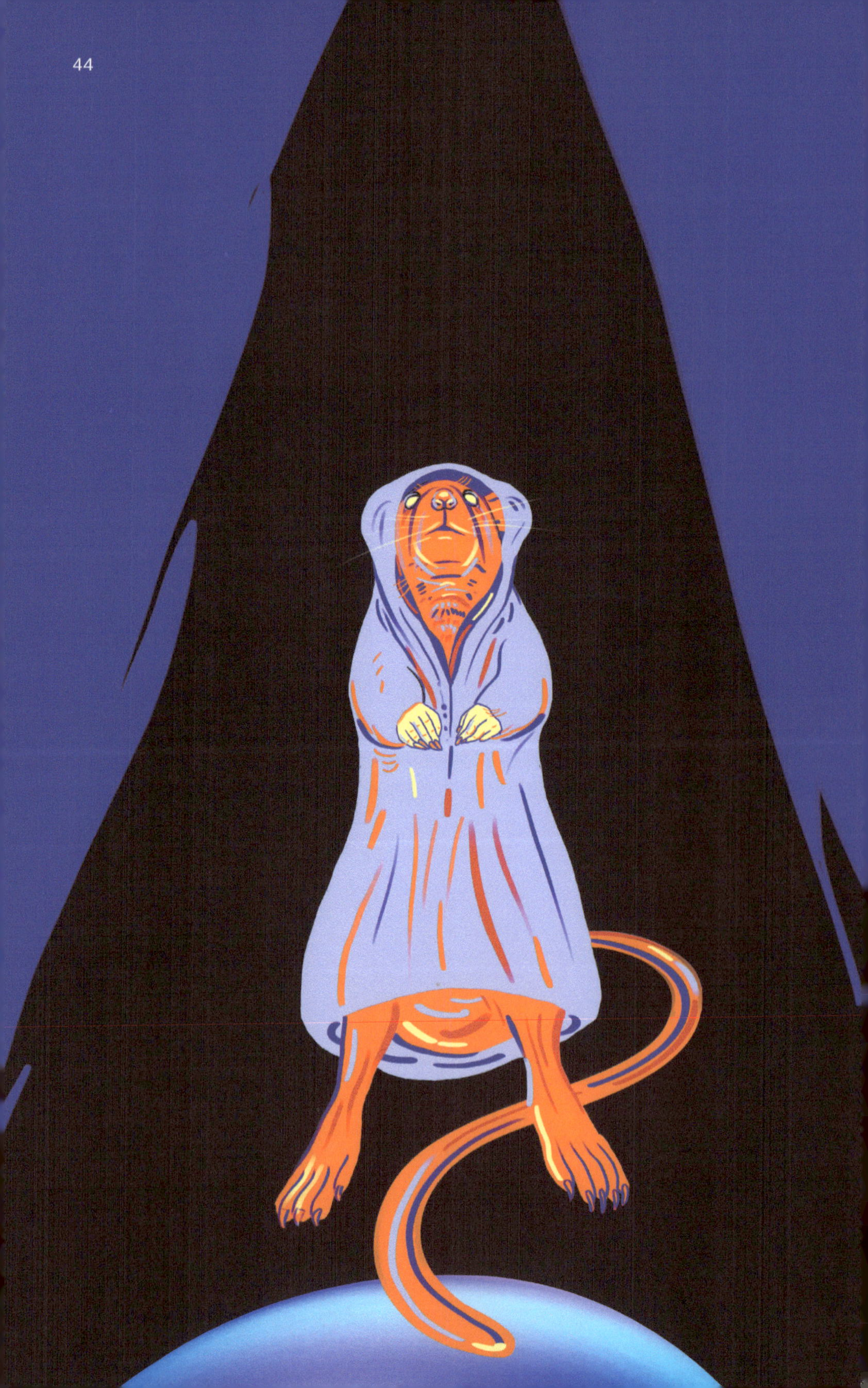

Now with the new reality cracking open,
what will happen to the 12 spirits that
have broken out from their old shackles?

The 12 Breaking Out Animals II
to be continued……

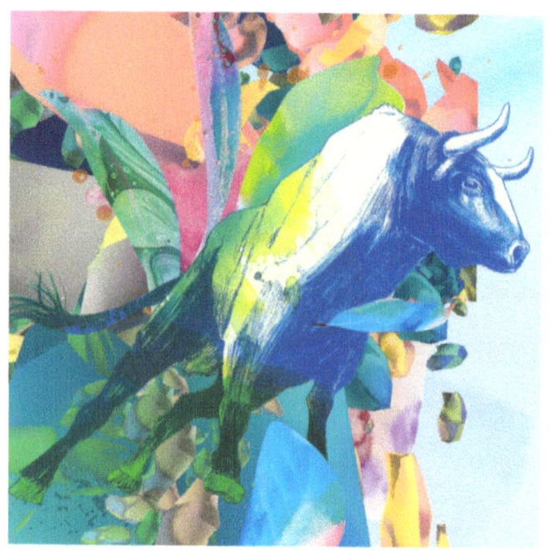

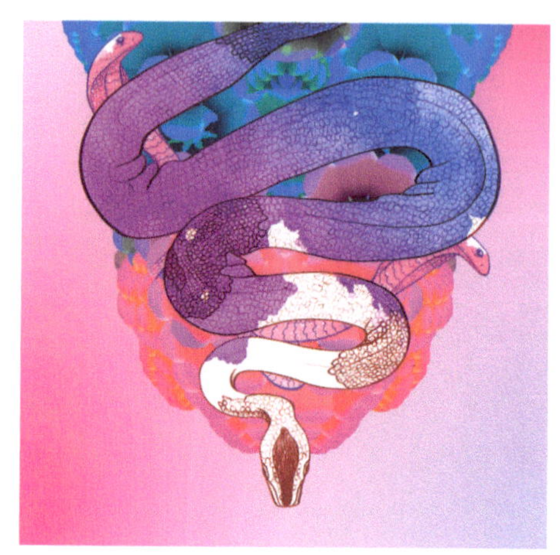

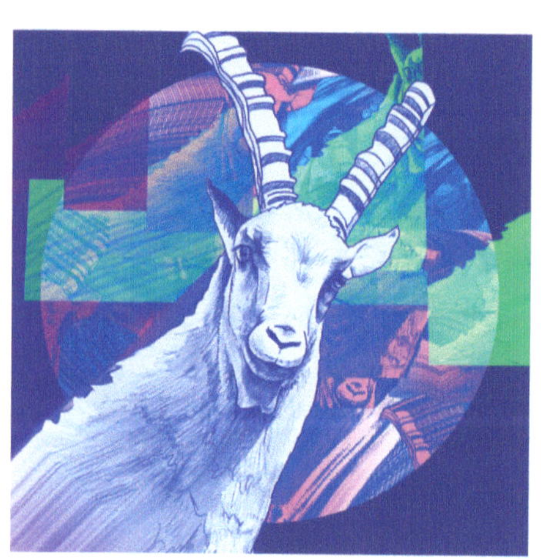

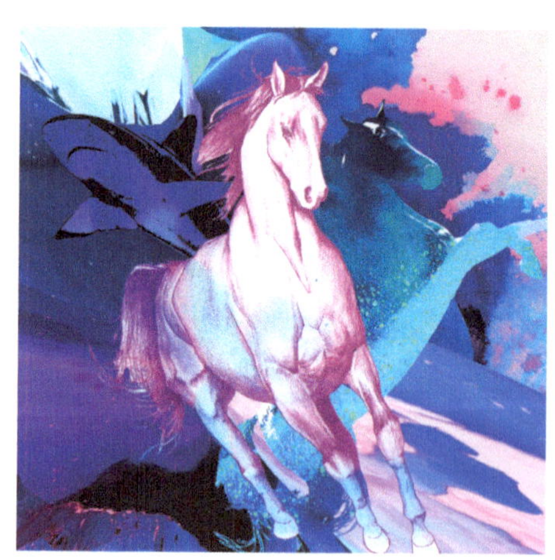

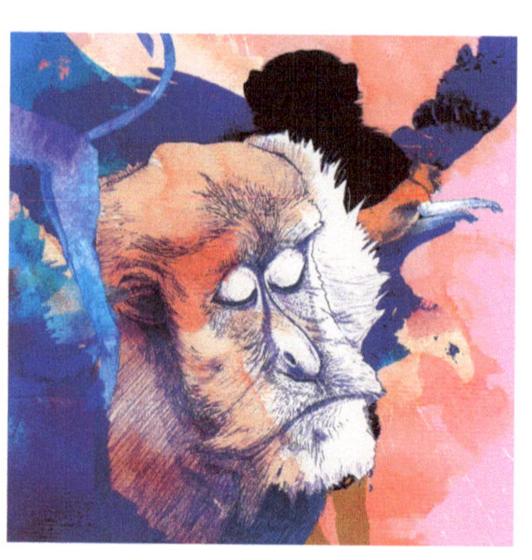

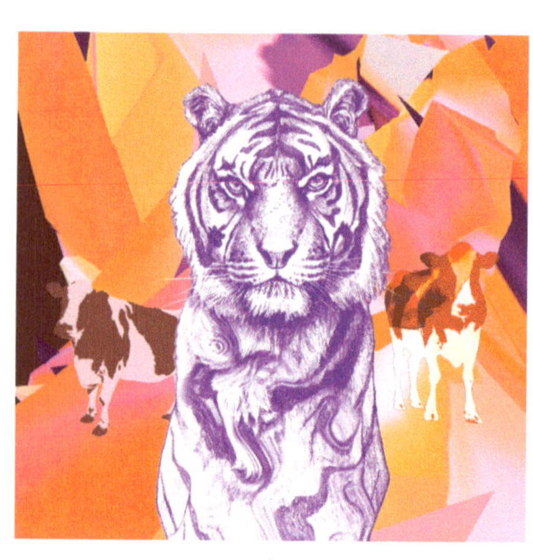

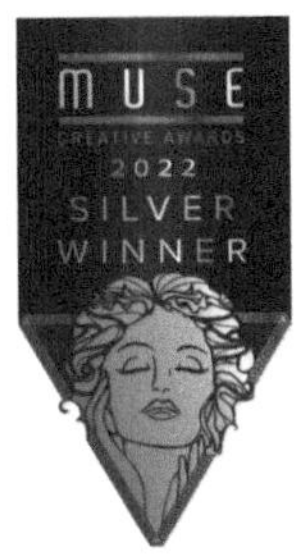

View the arworks
in Metaverse

www.t12boa.com

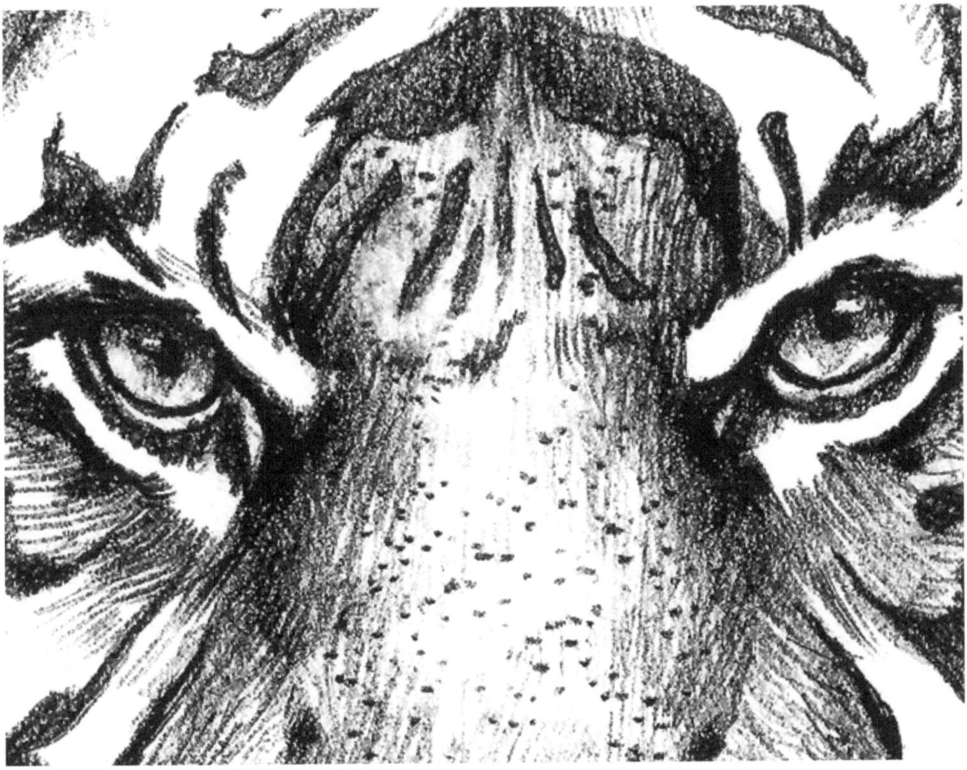

in Disguise

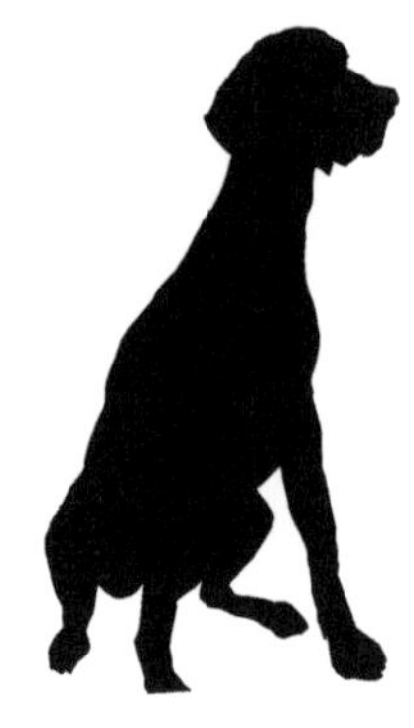

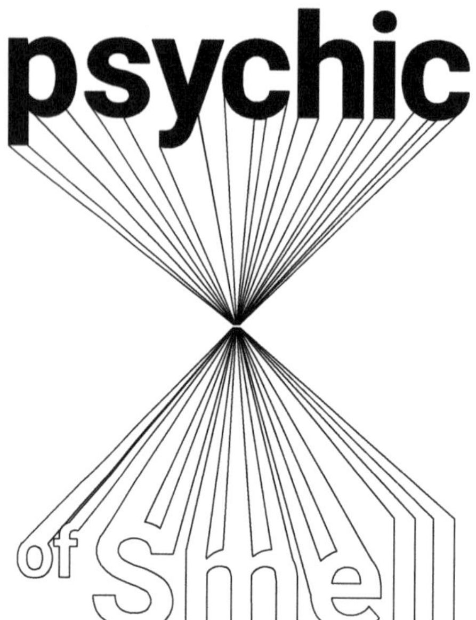

psychic of Smell

Wave Making

Cyber Surf

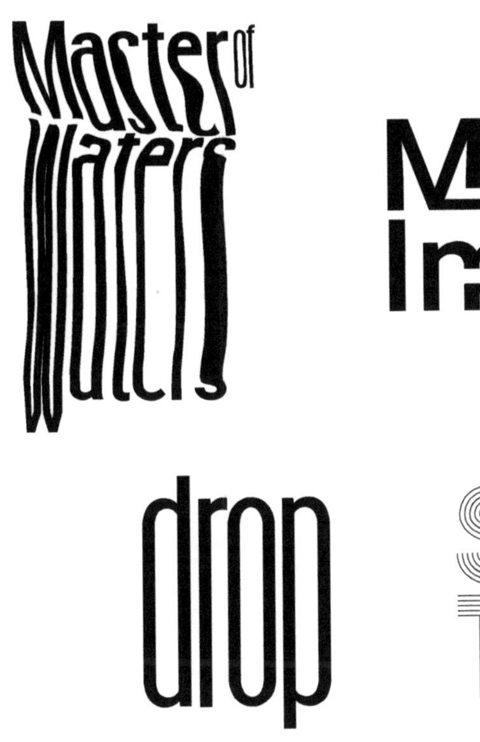

Master of Waters
Mind Imposer
drop
Shake Time

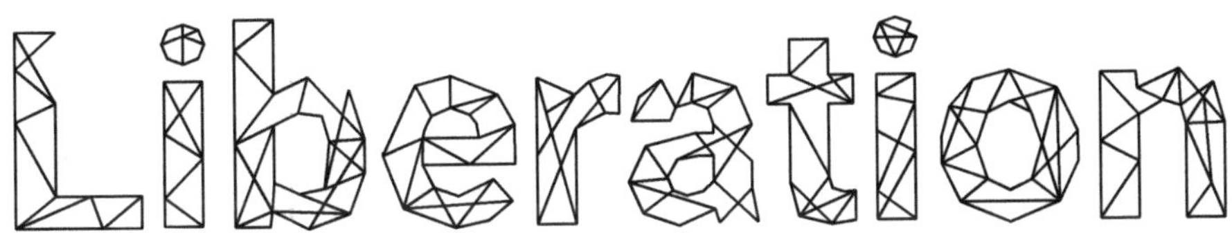

Liberation

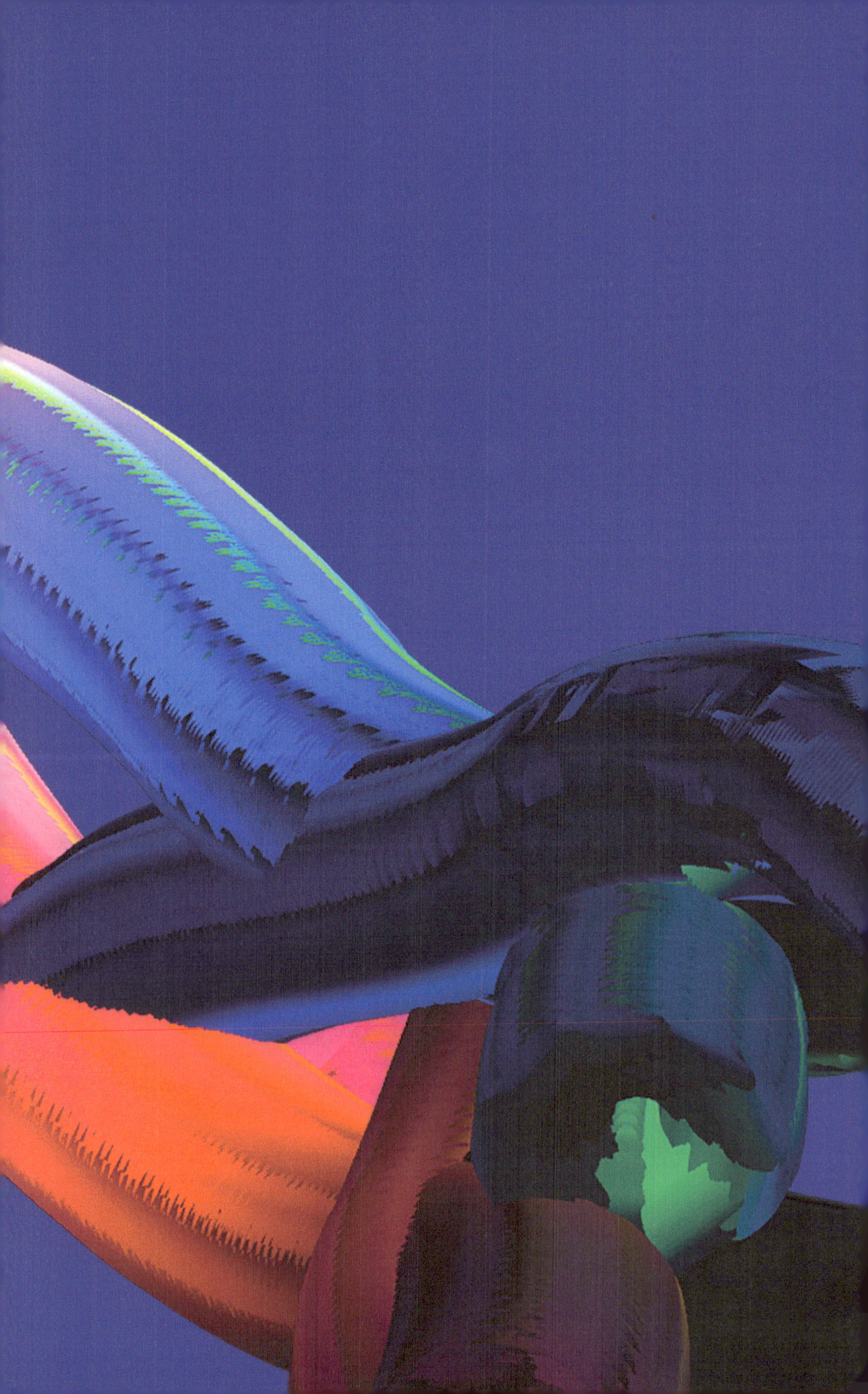

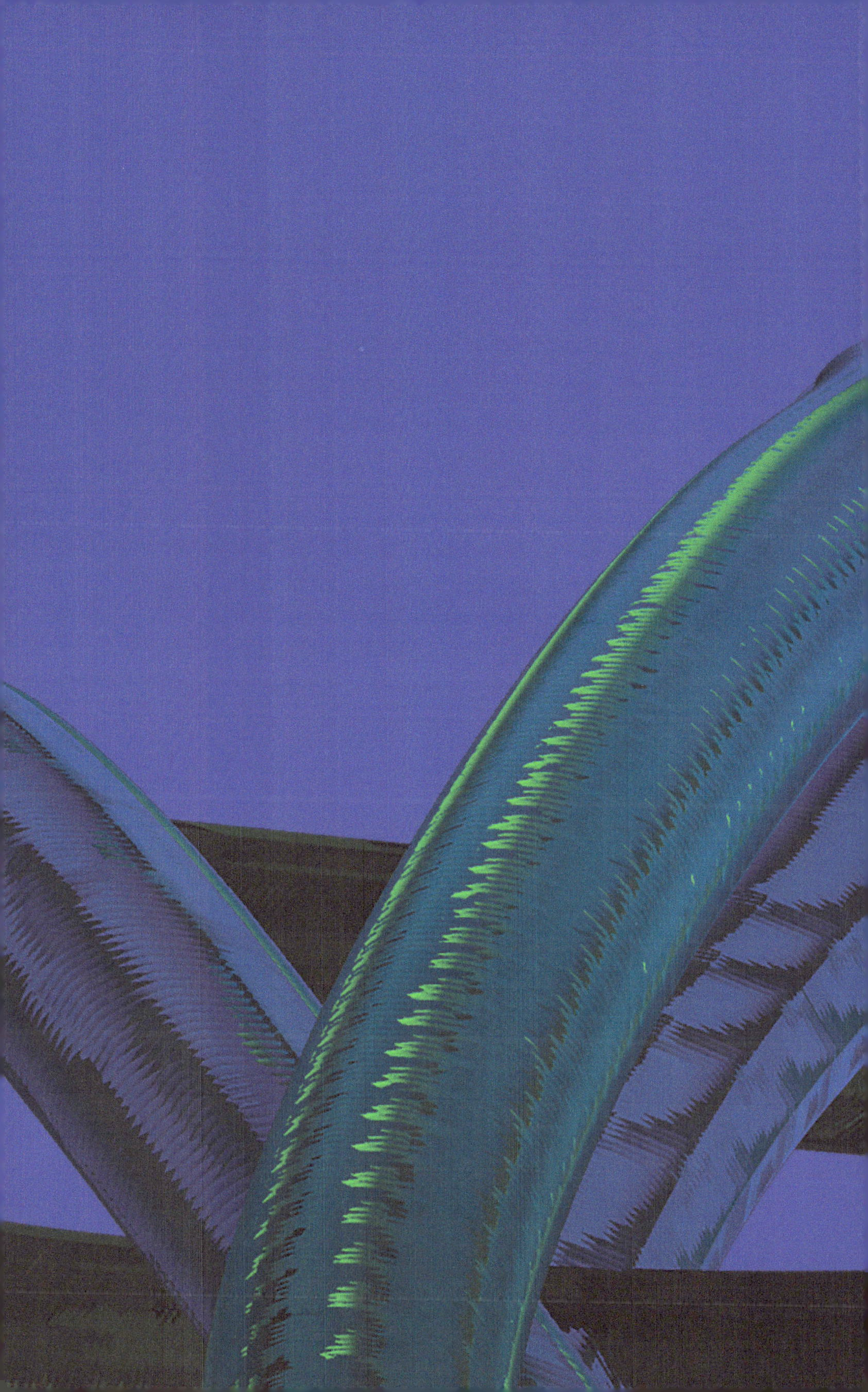